# Group Work

## Cybernetic, Constructivist, and Social Constructionist Perspectives

Raphael J. Becvar, Ph.D.
Northeast Louisiana University

Brian S. Canfield, Ed.D.
Northeast Louisiana University

Dorothy S. Becvar, M.S.W., Ph.D.
St. Louis Family Institute

**LOVE PUBLISHING COMPANY®**
Denver • London • Sydney

Published by Love Publishing Company
Denver, Colorado 80222

Library of Congress Catalog Card Number 96-78052

Copyright © 1997 Love Publishing Company
Printed in the U.S.A.
ISBN 0-89108-252-2

# Contents

# Preface

*T*he idea for this book was born as we reviewed several introductory textbooks on group work and became aware that none of them used systems theory, or cybernetics, constructivism, or social constructionism as an organizing framework.[1] To us, this situation was indeed interesting, for group work builds on theories of interpersonal relationships, which are the stuff of the cybernetic perspective and social constructionism. To remedy this gap in the literature, we set out to write this book.

The challenge seemed simple enough, that is, to explicate the theories of first-order and second-order cybernetics, constructivism, and social constructionism and then apply them to group work. Explicating the perspectives was a relatively easy task; the greater challenge, we found, involved applying them to group work. In effect, we sought to select those approaches and models most frequently associated with family therapy, stay consistent with the basic premises of the models, and apply them to working with groups. In this effort, we tended to be conservative. Indeed, readers may expand the boundaries of these models and, or, adapt them in different ways to fit more traditional conceptions of group work. For example, the generic principles of first-order cybernetics may be a useful conceptual map for thinking about group membership, group dynamics, the process of change, and the transfer of learning.

---

[1] Although a distinction can be made between systems theory and cybernetics, we use the term cybernetics in this text to include the concept of systems theory.

Group work takes many forms. However, we limited our discussion to those forms categorized as group therapy, therapy in groups, and one-to-one therapy in a group context. In our attempts at integration we found that some first-order cybernetic approaches to family therapy (e.g., those of Satir and Bowen) fit or could be adapted to fit all three categories. Yet, most second-order cybernetic and social constructionist approaches, or selected procedures from them, could be applied only to therapy in groups or to one-to-one therapy in groups without seriously violating some basic assumptions of those approaches. Indeed, in general, the idea of a "model" is philosophically inconsistent with the assumptions of social constructionism.

The fundamental tension we experienced was that between the modernist and postmodernist philosophical traditions. Mainstream group work literature and traditional mental health practice are more consistent with modernism than postmodernism, and the latter, as a philosophical tradition, challenges many of the assumptions of modernism, including traditional mental health practice and group work. In fact, therapy consistent with the postmodern tradition deconstructs much of mental health practice consistent with the modernist tradition.

As you read this book, you will become aware that we make relatively few references to the rich literature on group dynamics and group work. Rather, we take the position that group dynamics, stages of group development, and so forth, reflect the theoretical model used by the group leader. Thus, our citations are limited to those models and theories that fit or complement the models we have chosen to explicate.

We have divided this book into two parts. In Part One, which includes Chapters 1 and 2, we provide an explanation of first-order cybernetics, second-order cybernetics, constructivism, and social constructionism. In Part Two, in Chapters 3 through 7, we share thoughts and general therapeutic processes illustrative of how a group leader might think about group work and intervene given these three modes of thought. In Chapter 3, we present ways of thinking about group dynamics, group process, and group leadership, about the pragmatics of group work, and about leadership style that we feel are consistent with the frameworks of first-order cybernetics, second-order cybernetics, constructivism, and social constructionism. In Chapters 4, 5, and 6, we describe specific models consistent with each of these frameworks that were designed for family therapy or for work with individuals. We attempt to apply the basic ideas from these approaches to group work in a manner that is in accordance with the basic assumptions made by the authors of the models. However, at the same time, we acknowledge that the application of these ideas to group work is, by and large, our construction rather than that of the authors of the models. We assume responsibility for any inconsistency between our construction or application of a model and the intent of the author(s). We also present, in a manner consistent with our theoretical perspective, some activities that a leader might use in the context of a group to facilitate its development and the achievement of its goals. Finally, in Chapter 7, we review some issues that arise with the use of various perspectives. We also present ideas about what might be termed second-order ethics in group work, which emerge as a function of our particular theoretical orientation, and address evaluation and research issues.

As you read this book you may be challenged to examine some cherished notions about therapy in general and group work in particular. In addition, you may become more aware that although what therapists do in group therapy can be therapeutic, it also can be toxic. As a final note, although the primary focus of the book is on group work, you may find the ideas and activities presented useful for working with individuals, couples, families, or larger social systems. We hope that you find our contribution meaningful and enjoyable.

We would like to express our appreciation to Robert Conyne of the University of Cincinnati and Chuck Kormanski of the University of Pennsylvania, Altoona, who read an early version of the manuscript and made many helpful suggestions. We also appreciate the support of Stan Love and the fine work editing the manuscript by Kristin Kennedy and her assistants.

*Raphael J. Becvar, Brian S. Canfield, and Dorothy S. Becvar*

# *Part One*

## Philosophical and Theoretical Perspectives

*I*n Part One of this book, we explore some areas in the realm of philosophy and theory. In Chapter 1, we offer explanations of first-order cybernetics, second- or higher-order cybernetics, and constructivism. Then, in Chapter 2, we present a brief overview of the contrasting worldviews of modernism and postmodernism and a discussion of social constructionism. To us, the postmodern perspective provided by cybernetics, constructivism, and social constructionism opens the door to different and useful ways of thinking about ourselves, our relationships with one another, and our work as mental health professionals. Indeed, we find it offers the sort of resource to which Alan Watts referred when he noted that "problems that remain persistently insoluble should be suspected as questions asked in the wrong way" (Watts, 1972, p. 54). That is, the answers one receives depends upon the questions one asks. And as an individual becomes aware of and then examines the philosophical and theoretical assumptions underlying a particular perspective, he or she may find it possible to shift to a different perspective, one in which the "problem" is no longer a problem or the nature of the "problem" to be solved is changed. This view is consistent with Milton Erickson's (personal communication, July 14, 1978) view of his work: "People come with problems they can't solve. I give them problems they can solve." So, we begin with a consideration of some different ways to understand our world.

# 1

# Cybernetics and Constructivism

*C*ybernetic concepts can be described with relatively few propositions. That is, from a cybernetic perspective, everything—people, ideas, and things—in the universe is assumed to be connected. Thus, reality is not something "out there," independent of people. Rather, reality must necessarily include people and their ideas, and it takes the form of the ideas people use to describe it through language. Accordingly, our focus in a discussion of cybernetics is on relationships, patterns, and process, and we assume recursion, or circular causality. Although relatively few, assumptions such as these may be challenging inasmuch as they are more consistent with an Eastern rather than a Western worldview.

## First-Order Cybernetics

Societies, including their institutions and professions (e.g., teaching, parenting, family life education, therapy), all are organized to greater or lesser degrees within the parameters of the prevailing worldview of the members of that society. In American society, the idea of the autonomous individual, separate and independent, is a basic organizing assumption. It is this assumption that is challenged most basically by cybernetics.

In the behavioral sciences, for example, the individual traditionally has been understood as the fundamental unit of analysis. Thus, behavioral scientists have assumed as appropriate the model of the hard sciences, which for decades has sought to isolate and study the basic units or building blocks of matter. Accordingly, they have chosen to study the decontextualized monad, the autonomous individual or personality, and through that study have sought to understand the nature of the human mind. They have made the assumption, also consistent with the prevailing worldview, that by observation one can analyze, discover, and understand what is really going on with the individual. And what they have seen when they have looked at this isolated monad are "patients," "mental illness," and "causes" residing within individual minds. Accordingly, causes have taken the form of such things as volition, character traits, repression, and projections, to name just a few.

First-order cybernetics challenges such a stance by asking two simple questions: "How is it possible to understand an individual out of context?" and "How can an individual be studied apart from the world of which she or he is necessarily a part?" Thus, as it came of age in the field of family therapy, first-order cybernetics began to direct the attention of therapists and theorists to certain phenomena that did not fit the autonomous, independent person assumption. Therapists and theorists observed that people's behavior changes from one context to another. They noticed that people behave differently in different situations. Indeed, they recognized that a fundamental intention of all therapy is to create a context in which the thoughts, feelings, and behavior of people referred to as clients or patients can evolve and change. Thus, different theories of individual, family, and group counseling and therapy developed that suggest that different kinds of contexts may be created to evolve the particular kinds of changes desired.

In studies focused on the family, attempts to understand people necessitated that the unit of analysis be changed from the individual to how the various individuals related to one another. To study one apart from the other (parents, siblings, classmates, teachers, and so forth) would allow one to know that person relative to the new context (the context in which he or she is studied) but not in the context of his or her relationships. However, as Minuchin (1984, p. 72) noted, "Our culture promotes selfhood so we tend to blur our connections."

Once attention turned from the behavior of the autonomous individual to the context (not synonymous with environment) in which behavior occurs, researchers, theorists, and therapists shifted from an inferential study of the mind to a study of the observable manifestations of relationships. As described by Amatea and Sherrard (1994):

> Rather than looking atomistically at the person by dissecting his or her insides (i.e., psyche) to find the cause of his or her difficulties, first-order cybernetic systems thinkers look at both the intimate social network in which the individual is embedded and the more superordinate social network for clues to the relevant causal system supporting the problem. (pp. 9–10)

Theorists and therapists thus began to observe how two people in a relationship behaved with each other and how the behavior of each changed in the context of a third person, or a fourth person, or at a park, at home, at school, or at a ball game. The observers began to see redundant, or repeating, patterns of behavior between people. They also began to see that each person in a relationship was simultaneously the cause and the effect of the behavior of the other, the notion known as reciprocal causality. In addition, they became aware that if decontextualized individuals did not exist, then it logically followed that two people in a relationship also must be viewed in context. And so, researchers and theorists formulated the idea of nested systems, which stated that to understand the individual, one needs to understand him or her in the context of his or her family. (Keep in mind that the unit of analysis for family therapists was the family.) Further, to understand the family, one must understand it in the context of the community of which it necessarily is a part. And to understand the community, one must study it in the context of the city of which it necessarily is a part, and so on. Thus, the idea of a suprasystem evolved, which is the system of systems.

Although the suprasystem has, at times, been divided into subsystems for heuristic (and sometimes political) purposes, it is important to remember that the focal system, whether individual, couple, or family, continues to exist interdependently within a larger system. Indeed, as stated at the outset, from a cybernetic perspective, the universe is totally interconnected. Each component of a system is meaningful only in relationship to the other components of the system. Figures 1.1 and 1.2 illustrate this idea.

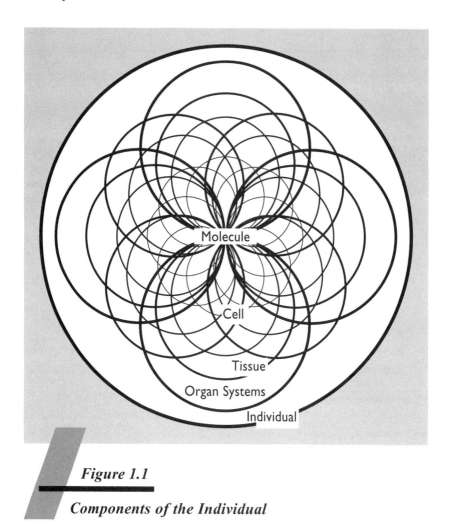

*Figure 1.1*

*Components of the Individual*

The idea of nested systems was a useful one, but it also led re-searchers to the understanding that there really is only one system, the suprasystem, which is the system of all possible subsystems that are components of it. Further, researchers became aware that (a) iso-lating a component (subsystem) of the larger system (suprasystem) for purposes of observation and understanding serves to provide in-formation about the subsystem out of the context of the larger system and (b) the system isolated for observation is a system only within one's conceptual model of what constitutes a system.

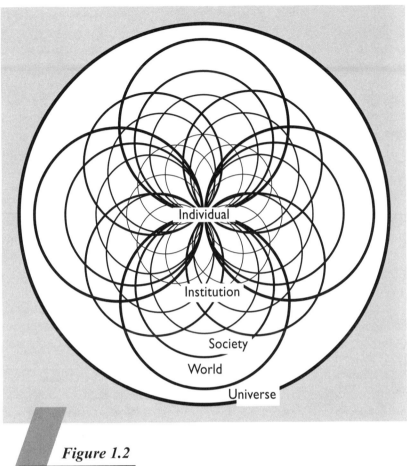

*Figure 1.2*

*Components of the Universe*

For family therapists and theorists, attention shifted from observations of individuals to observations of the redundant patterns of behavior in the family. Likewise, in this book we focus on observing and understanding the redundant patterns in peoples' lives, in their daily relationships as well as in the larger systems to which they belong.

Indeed, what is important from the cybernetic perspective is the assumption that by observing redundant patterns of behavior between components or persons in a system, one can arrive at some understanding of the nature of that system. That is, once two people meet, they quickly establish a predictable, stable pattern of behavior vis-à-vis one another. Each calibrates and choreographs his or her behavior in a manner that is consistent with the behavior of the other. Through their ongoing interaction, this pattern is continually reaffirmed or modified. This concept is called recursion, or the recursive organization of behavior. Moreover, with the concept of recursion, the concept of causality self-destructs; when it is referred to, it is viewed as reciprocal causality. Thus, the behavior of each person in a relationship influences and is influenced by the behavior of the other. Stated somewhat differently, the behavior of each is a logical complement to the behavior of the other.

The concept of reciprocal causality stands in contrast with that of linear causality, the usual way of thinking in contemporary Western society. In linear-causal thinking, *A* causes *B* (*A*————>*B*). From one person's point of view, "I defend because you criticize"; "I nag because you withdraw." From the point of view of the other, who also is thinking in a linear-causal manner, "I criticize because you defend"; "I withdraw because you nag." That is, with linear-causal thinking, neither person in a relationship sees his or her behavior as participating in creating or maintaining the behavior of the other, the behavior that each would like to see changed. However, in all relationships the role of one party is a logical complement to the role of the other, such as the prosecutor and the defendant, the teacher and the student. The role of each participates in creating and maintaining the role of the other. At the level of behavior, therefore, cyberneticians talk of sequences such as "attacking-defending," "nagging-withdrawing," and "listening-talking" as logical complements.

A related idea in the cybernetic perspective is that no role or behavior can maintain itself on its own energy—each role or behavior needs the logical complement of the other. Thus, one can continue in the role of teacher only as long as it is complemented by the role of student, and vice versa. The role of teacher cannot maintain itself without the complementary role of student. The infinity symbol is used to describe redundant patterns of behavior and the related concept of recursion or reciprocal causality in a relationship. For example:

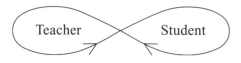

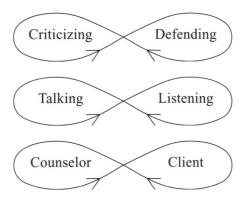

From this perspective, teacher behavior does not cause student behavior, nor does student behavior cause teacher behavior. Similarly, criticizing does not cause defending, and defending does not cause criticizing; talking does not cause listening, and listening does not cause talking. That is, neither half of the equation is the cause of the other. Rather, each is a necessary complement to, and participates in, the creation and maintenance of the other—hence, the phrase reciprocal causality.

Another way of stating this idea is to say that relationships are bilateral. It takes two to create a relationship, and both members participate in the creation of whatever evolves. If a person in a relationship feels that people are independent, autonomous, and substantive, he or she may attempt to change the other person in the relationship while remaining in a fixed position. However, attempts at unilateral change in a relationship that is bilateral must fail. Viewed systematically, if a person experiences an undesirable behavior in someone with whom he or she has a relationship, then that person must ask about his or her own behavior relative to the undesirable behavior. Indeed, one's attempts to change the other person in a relationship may participate in, indeed probably are, maintaining the behavior he or she would like to see change.

From a cybernetic perspective, the behavior of each person in a relationship constitutes feedback to the other. And it is in the context of the ongoing feedback between members that the stability of the relationship is maintained. In cybernetic terminology, behavior that logically complements the behavior of the other is referred to as negative feedback. Such feedback has nothing to do with behavior one might classify as unpleasant, nor does it necessarily constitute criticism.

Rather, it indicates that there is no change; it is used to describe the stability and continuing redundant pattern of logically complementary behavior in a relationship.

The concept of positive feedback is a complement to the concept of negative feedback. As with negative feedback, positive feedback does not refer to a value judgment, in this case about whether or not behavior that is experienced is good or pleasant. Rather, it refers to behavior that is new or different, that is, behavior that is not a logical complement to the behavior of the other. Further, it refers to only the first instance of a new, different, or illogical behavior.

As family therapists and theorists developed an understanding of how a system remains stable, they began also to understand how a system or relationship might change. That is, if any behavior or role needs a logical complement, then any behavior of one person that is not a logical complement to the behavior of the other must necessarily have an impact on the relationship. As previously noted, no behavior or role can maintain itself on its own energy—it needs a logical complement. The pattern of interaction in a relationship is stable as long as each person continues to act in a way that logically complements the behavior of the other. Therefore, if one wishes to change the redundant, reciprocal pattern of behavior in a relationship, one must behave in a way that is illogical; one must do something new or different. Further, if one acts in a way that is different or illogical to the behavior of the other in the relationship and maintains the new behavior, the behavior of the other cannot stay the same.

Thus, in this perspective, the idea of different or illogical behavior is the key to changing the redundant pattern of behavior in a relationship. Consider a relationship marked by criticism. A logical complement of criticism is defensive behavior. Another logical complement of criticism is criticism about the criticism. Crying and pleading to stop the criticism are also logical complements. All participate in maintaining the current pattern of behavior in the relationship; all are more of the same kinds of responses in that each makes sense in the context of, or is a logical attempt to stop, the criticism. Conversely, illogical or different behavior in response to criticism might include complimenting the other on the variety of ways he or she criticizes; thanking the other for his or her concern and desire to help; and "acting crazy," such as by becoming catatonic, singing a song, dancing about the room, speaking about things that have no logical connection to the conversation from the perspective of the person who is criticizing. Indeed, some family systems theorists began to see that what has been called "crazy" behavior in the context of a destructive and contradictory pattern of behavior in a relationship might be understood as a creative and often ingenious way of breaking the redundant pattern of behavior in the relationship (Bateson, 1972).

As the focus of study shifted from the monad or decontextualized individual to the interaction patterns between persons, the concern shifted to what is going on rather than why it is happening. Watzlawick (1990, p. 17) described the difference between these two approaches as follows: "From a monadic viewpoint we ask about reason, cause, motive, in other words, why? From a pragmatic standpoint we ask what is happening in the here and now." By studying patterns between people in the here and now and by moving away from asking why, researchers began to see that the system may be its own best explanation. That is, how the system reached a particular point is not relevant even if one could know. There are many possible explanations regarding cause, all of them plausible. Further, no matter how the system reached its current position, the end point is equally final (called equifinality, or that's where it is and that's the way it is). Similarly, the system has equal potential (called equipotentiality) for new patterns of redundant and reciprocal behavior relative to the ability of the people in it to interrupt or otherwise change their behavior relative to the other.

With a "here and now" focus on redundant and reciprocal patterns of behavior, one looks at the interactions between two persons in a relationship as a whole, that is, as a system in its own right. Together, people in relationship constitute one organism. Again, understanding the nature of each individual in a relationship independent of the others in the relationship does not provide information about the nature of the relationship. For, the whole is greater than the sum of its parts, a concept known as nonsummativity. In the physical world, for example, "Water is more and different from the mere summation of the properties of hydrogen and oxygen" (Watzlawick, 1990, p. 20). Similarly, in the relationship system composed of, for example, Mary and Harold, $1 + 1 = 3$. That is, Mary is one component, Harold is the second component, and their redundant patterns of interaction form the third component. If there were three people in the system, the equation would have to take into account person $A$, person $B$, person $C$, their relationships with each other (three relationships), which describes

a triangle. Hence, in a three-person system there are seven components. Watzlawick (1990) summarized the implications of this shift
in thinking from the monad to the relationship as follows:

> As long as human behavior is examined monadically, ... we speak of
> 'patients,' 'mental illness,' and so forth. It is one of our hypotheses that
> there are disturbed relationships but not disturbed individuals or, to put
> it more precisely, that behavior disorders are a function of human rela-
> tionships but not of sick minds. (p. 21)

In addition, from this perspective, when researchers talk about
observing redundant and reciprocal patterns of behavior, they really
are talking about observing patterns of communication. That is, the
concept of a relationship between two people implies communication.
Thus, observers of a relationship direct their attention to the interactions between the people involved.

When people think of communication, they usually think about
words, which can also be referred to as symbols, or the digital level
of communication. And as people focus on words, they usually think
of a sender and a receiver who take turns sending and receiving. However, in a relationship, the distinction between sender and receiver
gets fuzzy when one considers nonverbal, or analog, behavior. Indeed,
it is possible to not communicate verbally. However, one cannot not
communicate at the nonverbal level.

Thus, in the cybernetic perspective, all behavior in the context of
a relationship is communication, and one cannot not behave. All behavior is communication. Moreover, nonverbal behavior is defined as
a more powerful form of communication than other types of behavior. It is often referred to as the command level, for the nonverbal
message influences how the verbal message is to be interpreted. It
always qualifies and modifies the verbal communication. In other words,
nonverbal behavior, or communication, is meta to (above or about)
the explicit content of the verbal message. Thus, it is called
metacommunication. It is also called the relationship-defining aspect
of communication. For example, the phrase "I love you" communi-
cates something quite different when said angrily than when said lov-
ingly. The message received is relative to the nonverbal component
(tone of voice, posture, focus of attention, mannerisms, and so forth).
Accordingly, nonverbal behavior contextualizes the verbal. However,
the nonverbal, or analogic, level also includes the setting, the percep-

tions of those in the setting, and the context in which the communication behavior occurs. Thus, the statement, "The trash is piling up," made in the kitchen in the presence of a 12-year-old son will be interpreted very differently than the same statement said in the same tone of voice in the context of a city landfill in the presence of the same 12-year-old son. In the latter case, it is doubtful that the words would be taken as a command to the son to take out the trash, an interpretation that is highly likely in the former setting.

Pragmatically, the cybernetic perspective changes the way one thinks about people. To summarize, some of the basic principles of systems theory at the level of first-order cybernetics include the following:

1. One cannot not behave.
2. All behavior is communication.
3. One cannot not communicate.
4. Communication has two components: digital, or verbal, and analog, or nonverbal plus context.
5. Nonverbal behavior contextualizes, or is meta to, verbal behavior and composes the command or relationship-defining aspect of communication.
6. Context is meta to both verbal and nonverbal communication.
7. People are not simply the way they are independent of context (that is, substantively); they are the way they are as a function of a given context (that is, their behaviors are contextually relative). People are not simply specific kinds or types of persons, they are the way they are with others as a function of the way others are with them. Each is a part of the context of the other.
8. When contexts change and the new context is maintained, the behavior of people in a relationship changes. Likewise, when the behavior of one person in a relationship changes and this new behavior is maintained, the behavior of the other person in the relationship cannot stay the same.
9. Attempts by one person to change the behavior of another person (an effort that makes sense from a trait and type psychology) while staying the same will not only not change that behavior but will maintain and perhaps participate in the escalation of the problem behavior.

10. Behavior labeled as problematic (mad or bad) is "normal" or a part of the natural ecology in the context of a given relationship. Correspondingly, behavior labeled as good also is "normal" or a part of the natural ecology in the context of a given relationship.

11. No behavior can maintain itself on its own energy; it needs a logical complement.

12. Behaving in a way that is illogical or different will break the redundant, reciprocal pattern by which a relationship may be characterized.

13. From the cybernetic perspective, observers do not think in terms of why, or of linear causality; if they speak of cause, they think in terms of recursion, reciprocal causality, or mutual influence.

14. The whole is greater than the sum of the parts, or $1 + 1 = 3$.

15. The system is its own best explanation. The system is what it is and does what it does.

16. In attempts to understand a system, the focus is on current behavior in the here and now.

17. Attempts to understand "individuals" out of context are not useful because people always exist in some context. That to which a person necessarily belongs has no outside for that person.

18. One's identity or sense of self is defined relative to the context of the relationships of which that person is a part. Thus, there is no unified singular sense of self. Instead, there are multiple selves that one experiences in the context of different relationships.

# Second- or Higher-Order Cybernetics and Constructivism

Grounded in first-order cybernetics, the field of family therapy was built on the idea of understanding natural systems. Thus, theorists and therapists attempted to observe and discover what was going on "out there" in the family or in whatever relationship they targeted. And they began to develop elaborate theories to describe the redundant patterns they believed they had discovered in the families under observation.

This enterprise was exciting for those involved, and it was believed that great progress was being made through seeking to understand human behavior in the context of the family, the community, the nation, and so forth. However, as explanations evolved relative to the assumption of an interconnected universe, a problem was encountered. The problem pointed to an inconsistency in the logic of the theory. Although a totally interconnected universe was assumed, the observers were excluding themselves as they "observed" and "discovered" what was "out there"; they were acting as though they as "scientists" (observers, teachers, principals, counselors, parents) were not part of a world in which everything and everyone is connected. They positioned themselves on the outside of the system and believed they could observe without influencing the system being observed.

In essence, they were saying that everything in the universe was connected except themselves. As a result of their belief, the observers punctuated themselves as separate from that which they were observing. Accordingly, first-order cybernetics implies that the observer is independent of the system being observed. However, the idea that people can remain independent of a system they are observing becomes untenable if proponents of the cybernetic perspective are to be consistent with themselves. Given this dilemma, the next question was, how do people observe and understand a system of which they as observers are necessarily a part? The answer came in the form of a new concept, second- or higher-order cybernetics, also known as cybernetics of cybernetics (Keeney, 1982, 1983).

Second-order cybernetics suggests that observers must include themselves in the system they are attempting to observe, the idea of the participant-observer. Accordingly, proponents of the perspective assume that the act of observing affects the things and people being observed in ways that inevitably "distort" the "real nature" of those things and people. The same observation was made in the "hard science" of quantum mechanics as early as the 1920s (Briggs & Peat, 1984; Capra, 1983; Hayward, 1984). Paradoxically, the "real nature" of someone or something can be defined only in relationship to oneself as observer, and through this relationship a new and different "real nature" evolves.

So, what is it that observers see when they observe themselves observing the systems of which they are necessarily a part? They see what their construction of the worldview of their society suggests is "out there." Society creates the box (worldview, or ecology of ideas) and guides their viewing of phenomena as a function of those beliefs to which they subscribe. Thus, by putting themselves as viewers inside the system, they see what they believe, and in that seeing they confirm the validity of their beliefs and the worldview of their society. In effect, observers look in a mirror and see themselves looking in a mirror (Briggs & Peat, 1984).

So, observations are not made from a blank slate that is value- and concept-free. Rather, people observe with preconceptions that are guided by values. Indeed, the act of observing implies a preconception about how one can know. Thus, proponents of second-order cybernetics entered the world of epistemology, or the study of how one can know what one knows. Not surprisingly, cyberneticians began to see that what one believed was out there was indeed out there. Thus, to the idea of seeing is believing, they added the idea that believing is seeing:

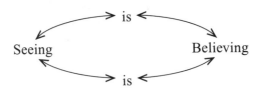

Discovery is an appropriate term to describe what observers do if they are separate from and independent of what they are observing, if they have no preconceptions of what they are observing, and if they can observe without transforming, perturbing, and evolving a different nature of things by the very act of observing. However, if observers believe that something is "out there," they will see it, and by seeing it their belief that it is "out there" will be confirmed. Further, different observers "discover" different things relative to the "out there" they believe exists. Thus, several questions arise: Which of the different versions of "out there" is the real "out there"? Does it make a difference which of the many available versions of "out there" one chooses to believe? Could it be that the "out there" one believes exists becomes "real" by the very act of believing in it and acting on the basis of this belief? Given this change in perspective and its related questions, cyberneticians found it necessary to let go of the idea of an "objective" person, family, or community.

Essentially, second-order cybernetics brought a constructivist perspective (von Glasersfeld, 1984) to systemic thinking. For, as Hoffman

(1993, p. 34) stated, "Constructivism holds that the structure of our nervous systems dictates that we can never know what is 'really' out there." Further, as Gale and Long (1995, p. 13) stated, "The two basic principles of radical constructivism are 1) knowledge is actively constructed by the individual and not passively received; and 2) the function of cognition organizes the experiential world rather than seeks to discover ontological reality." Thus, the "observed system" notion that one can know the truth about people (as well as other phenomena in the world) in any objective way self-destructs. Rather, all that observers can know is their construction of people and other world phenomena.

In other words, knowledge is actively constructed by the individuals doing the knowing. Although a real reality somewhere out there is not denied by such a stance, the stance does deny the possibility of a "true" representation of that reality. Von Glasersfeld (1979) elaborated as follows:

> We thus redefine "knowledge" as pertaining to invariances in the living organism's experience rather than to entities, structures and events in an independently existing world. Correspondingly, we redefine "perception." It is not the reception or duplication of information that is coming in from outside, but rather the construction of invariances by means of which the organism can assimilate and organize its experience. (p. 39)

Thus, the individual actively constructs cognitions as a function of his or her structure, which through accommodation and assimilation facilitates adaptation. The issue is one of survival, or of "not fatally colliding with the environment" (Hoffman, 1993, p. 37). Accordingly, the mind is understood as an "evolving, adapting organism" (Gale & Long, 1995, p. 13), and the individual, including the social scientist and the mental health professional, can know only his or her constructions of others and the world.

In effect, when one moves into the world of constructivism, one moves into the world of narratives or stories. In that perspective, a story is a set of explanatory concepts that describe a person's connections between him- or herself and others, as well as other creatures and things in his or her world. Thus, the concept of story describes the limits of what one can know. One cannot know the real nature of one's connections with others and the environment. All a person can know are his or her constructions. Further, a multiplicity of stories is possible for any person. Different stories describe different kinds of relationships as well as the different worlds in which people live relative to the stories they tell themselves about themselves and others.

A central implication of constructivism is that the idea of a "pathology" as an independent reality "out there" is untenable. Instead, pathology, or behavior that is viewed as maladaptive rather than adaptive, is created by one's use of diagnostic categories. Thus, there are no "objectively treatable structures" in individuals, couples, or families. Rather, the choice of a diagnostic category for individual or family dysfunction says more about the observer (observing system) than it does about what is really going on in the family or individual.

Accordingly, the basic tenets of first-order cybernetics about systems, as described previously, must be understood as "observed-system" constructions of the observer. Further, diagnostic categories, such as those of the DSM-IV (American Psychiatric Association, 1994), as well as the various models of dysfunctional families provided by different family therapy theories, cannot be considered to provide information about "objectively treatable structures." We do not mean to say that therapeutic interventions consistent with any of these "stories" will necessarily be ineffective for eliminating problematic behavior. However, as science philosopher Longino (1990) noted:

> That a theory works, that it can be used to predict correctly the empirical consequences either of naturally occurring events or of human interaction and manipulation of events in nature, is often taken as a reason for accepting it. But accepting a theory for practical or instrumental purposes and asserting it to be true are quite different acts. *"Working"* is not an epistemological notion. [emphasis added, p. 93]

With the shift to a higher-order cybernetics and constructivist stance in which the observer must include him- or herself in that which is observed, it became necessary to give up the idea of certainty and the assumption that one's search will end in "truth." The idea of the certainty of uncertainty had to be accepted. For any individual, the idea of uncertainty may be disconcerting, but it opens the door to many possibilities for creating new stories within which one can live one's life. For in creating new stories people may create new realities in the systems to which they belong.

For therapists following this perspective, the selection of a theory about the client system becomes one not of an "accurate diagnosis" but rather of a search for a story that will structurally couple, or fit, with the internal structure, or nervous system, of a particular client and in so doing will participate in creating a change such that the problem behavior is eliminated. Consistent with constructivism, the concept of structural determinism suggests that the environment does not determine the behavior of the client. Rather, the client's internal structure determines the behaviors of which he or she is capable. Moreover, the decision about which story will structurally couple with the client cannot be made in advance or independent of the client. It must evolve in the process of dialogue with members of the client system. Accordingly, instructional interactions with a client will not be successful unless they fit the client's structure.

From this framework, the "fit" of an intervention with the structure of the client is assumed to have occurred if the client system changes. Further, the degree and direction of change is recognized to be limited by the structure of the client and cannot be predicted. That is, there is no way to get inside, or know, another person's experience or structure. Moreover, clients may not "know" their own structure or experience. Thus, although it is possible to predict that change will occur, one cannot predict what it will look like. In cybernetic theory, this concept is referred to as a stochastic process, or randomness within the limits of what is possible.

The therapist who works from this framework attempts to become as "client-centered" as possible. Ideally, he or she shuts down any natural inclination to think in terms of a theory while listening to clients. At the same time, he or she is aware that the observing system stance acknowledges the inevitability of editing while listening and observing. Further, the therapist is aware that the questions he or she asks, as well as the material he or she chooses for mirroring, paraphrasing, or empathizing, cannot help but influence the nature of the stories the members of a client system present. Indeed, there are no true synonyms, for each "synonym" provides a slightly different shade of meaning that influences a story the client tells. Further, the stories clients tell are relative to a particular audience.

And so, in this discussion we have moved from a story about a science of discovery that ultimately reveals the real nature of people to a story that states that the nature of people depends upon the observers', and the people's, beliefs. Thus, as Plas (1986, p. 81) stated, "The absolute, one, true reality of life can never be an important issue from a systemic point of view. Rather, it is recognized that a multiplicity of tales is possible." Further, Plas noted, "The notion of the story is the umbrella idea for systemic psychology.... As we talk of stories rather than 'reality,' we are reminded that it is not possible anywhere or anytime to speak truth in the positivist, Western sense of that term. The truth we speak from a systemic point of view is a contextual truth" (p. 82).

Indeed, people are connected, and the nature of the connection or relationship people have with one another depends upon the stories they tell themselves about one another. At a fundamental level, the cybernetic perspective shatters the notion that the ecology of ideas or stories in one's cultural worldview describes "reality." It is but a map, and no map describes the territory (Korzybski, 1958). Direct knowledge of the territory will never be available to anyone—no one has a God's-eye view of the world (Bronowski, 1978). It is impossible to speak of truth; one can speak only of stories. Further, the stories people tell themselves about a situation or person strongly affect the way they relate to the situation or person. As we stated elsewhere,

> According to the notion of a storied reality, the form of our relationships with self, others, and creatures and things necessarily takes the form of the way we story ourselves and others. If we story the personality as residing solely within the person, we describe a relationship with a person who is independent of our participation. If we story the biblical "dominion over" rather than "stewardship" relative to nature we create a very different relationship with the other creatures and things in the world. If we story a "survival of the fittest" concept of evolution, then we story a social Darwinism in which some cultures/creatures are superior to others. If we story either/or rather than both/and, we establish polarities. (Becvar & Becvar, 1996, pp. 348–349)

The implications—for life in one's family, school, mental health practice, community, and world—of a move to higher-order cybernetics and constructivist thinking are profound. A partial list of those implications is presented below. That is, if a person were to operate from this perspective, that person would:

1. See herself as a part of the context of other people in her life and not as an independent observer of them.
2. Be aware that how these others "are" is relative to how she is with them, and vice versa, and that how she is with them depends upon the stories she tells herself about them and the stories they tell themselves about her.

3. Recognize that there is no "objective" observer of a phenomenon, and that by the act of observation people see what they believe to be "out there."

4. Be aware that if she believes a certain phenomenon is "out there," not only will she see it, but the act of observation will transform the phenomenon toward a form consistent with her belief.

5. Be aware that if she thinks within the same stories that define a phenomenon as a "problem," she will be stuck with attempted solutions that are logically consistent with those stories and hence probably will not only not solve the problem but also may participate in escalation and reification of the problem.

6. Be aware that any metaphor she or others uses to describe a person, as well as any actions she makes as though the metaphor describes the "real" person, will influence the person to demonstrate behavior that logically fits the metaphor. Moreover, in the process, the metaphor may lose its identity as metaphor and become reality.

7. Have an awareness that no story is or can be demonstrated to be "true," and thus she must speak of a multiverse of perspectives rather than of a universe.

8. Experience the excitement that emerges when she realizes that all that is available to her is the certainty of uncertainty, given that no story can be demonstrated to be the "true" story or the way a situation or person "really is."

9. Recognize that however disconcerting uncertainty may feel, it opens the door to possibilities of a new "story" that may better solve problems otherwise considered to be unsolvable.

10. Gain a conscious awareness of her potential, as well as the potential of those with whom she lives and works, as a result of expanding the boundaries of the box that is the worldview of her society.

# 2

## The Postmodernist and Social Constructionist Perspectives

*B*oth constructivism and social constructionism are based on the assumption that although there may be a real world "out there," one can never know that world in any absolute way. As noted in Chapter 1, constructivism is rooted in biology, the scientific study of individual perception, and the study of the human understanding of experience. Thus, the focus of constructivism is on what goes on within the individual. By contrast, social constructionism, which we explain in this chapter, evolved from community philosophy and community processing. From this perspective, reality is understood as a group phenomenon that evolves through language and dialogue. Indeed, an important part of social constructionism is the belief that a society creates an ecology of ideas that not only make up the mores of that society but also serves a social control function. According to the social constructionist perspective, one's experience is not his or her own. Additionally, social constructionists believe that all human experience is monitored for political, sociological, and psychological correctness. They believe that people monitor each other; professionals or agents of the society provide categories and concepts, which are viewed as "real" and not as constructions. This view emerged in the context of what is referred to as the postmodern philosophical tradition as exemplified by the social criticism of Michael Foucault

(1975, 1977), who analyzed both power and the restricted worldviews of the modernist philosophical tradition. We therefore contrast modernism and postmodernism as a prelude to presenting the social constructionist perspective.

# Modernism and Postmodernism

Modernism, as well as the related perspective of structuralism, is associated with a realist epistemology according to which one assumes the possibility of achieving objective knowledge of the world. Closely aligned with empiricist, positivist, reductionistic, and rationalist orientations, proponents of this perspective seek universal codes, patterns, and essences that exist "out there," independent of observers. The goal is to discover, map, and know the objective truth of the world of human behavior.

The modernist perspective provides the foundation for the traditional, normative social science and mental health practice in which the characteristics of healthy and unhealthy, functional and dysfunctional, and normal and abnormal individuals, couples, and families are studied. Modernists seek universal truths that they believe transcend differences in cultures and societies through "systematic observation and rigorous reasoning" (Gergen, 1991, p. 29). Further, in the modernist tradition, language is viewed as representational; that is, it is understood as reporting on what is "discovered" out there.

Such a view describes the world of the therapist as expert who takes charge of and sets the goals for therapy. This world is the same as that of first-order cybernetics—a world of assessment, diagnosis, and the treatment of problems as described by the DSM-IV, or by the categories that define dysfunctional couples and families. Accordingly, as we wrote elsewhere, "The therapist seeks, discovers, and treats the 'real' problem, the underlying structural flaw that is built into the system and which necessarily gives rise to symptoms" (Becvar & Becvar, 1996, p. 144). Indeed, we, therapists and social scientists

learned to rely on the power of science and the knowledge of objective experts who supposedly possess the truth about a reality which is out there, and which can be represented accurately and understood via reliable research data. Further, we trusted that we were progressing toward a greater good through the creation of ever more significant technological advances. Consistent with this tradition, the role of therapist and social scientist has been that of the social engineer. (Becvar & Becvar, 1996, p. 87)

Thus, social scientists in the modernist tradition conduct research to ascertain the characteristics of healthy individuals, couples, and families. And therapists as social engineers intervene to socialize clients into the definition of health defined by the research evidence of the social scientists.

The postmodernist perspective, which first found expression in the fields of sociology, semiotics, literary deconstruction, and communication theory, challenges the ideas as well as the possibility, of objective knowledge and absolute truth. Postmodernists assume that "reality" is inevitably subjective and thus question at a fundamental level the search for universal truths, structures, and essences. Further, consistent with higher-order cybernetics, postmodernists assume that people live in a reality made up of socially constructed and socially sanctioned narratives. Rather than inhabiting a universe, people, according to this perspective, dwell in a multiverse that is created through the act of observation.

Postmodernism also challenges the idea of therapists and social scientists as the possessors of "expert knowledge" or the "final word" (Hoffman, 1993). For postmodernists, the idea of having "expert knowledge" legitimizes the practice of social engineering and necessarily disempowers consumers. Indeed, an important part of the social engineering thrust of modernism is the socialization of people into an almost worshipful attitude toward science. That is, professionals who promote the myth of naturalism suggest that living, parenting, "marriaging," and "familying" should not be trusted to the untrained. Rather, according to the myth of professionalism, consumers are encouraged to look to the experts for knowledge and guidance regarding how to live their lives. Thus, "expert knowledge" equals power. Indeed, the two concepts are inseparable, as Foucault (1979, pp. 27–28) noted when he wrote, "Power produces knowledge.... There is no power in relation without the correlative constitution of a field of knowledge, nor any knowledge that does not presuppose and constitute at the same time, power relations."

# Social Constructionism

Social constructionism is closely aligned with the postmodern philosophical tradition. The social constructionist understands ordinary people and clients to possess equally valid perspectives and believes there is no "transcendent criterion of the correct" (Gergen, 1991, p. 111). Rather, knowledge within a culture is understood to be consensual and embedded in language. As Watts (1972, p. 64) wrote, "Our most private thoughts and emotions are not actually our own. For we think in terms of languages and images which we did not invent, but which were given to us by our society." For the social constructionist, such languages and images are in fact provided by the experts in various fields whose roles are sanctioned by what Becker (1967) called the "superordinate groups in the society." He referred to this ordering of society as a "hierarchy of credibility," which he described as follows:

> In any system of ranked groups, participants take it as a given that members of the highest group have the right to define the way things really are.... From the point of view of the well-socialized participant in the system, any tale told by those at the top intrinsically deserves to be regarded as the most credible account obtainable.... And since...matters of rank and status are contained in the mores, the belief has moral quality. We are, if we are proper members of the group, morally bound to accept the definitions imposed on the reality by the superordinate group in preference to the definitions espoused by subordinates.... By refusing to accept the hierarchy of credibility, we express disrespect for the entire established order. (p. 241)

Thus, social constructionists see the relationship between knowledge and power in the modernist reliance on an empiricist science that is controlled by superordinate groups of researchers and other professionals and that necessarily subjugates and disempowers subordinate groups. Such subordinate groups include, among others, women, people of color, people with different sexual orientations from the majority, people of minority cultures and ethnic groups, and people in poverty. Further, social constructionists believe that science, in the modernist tradition, seeks to reduce thinking as much as possible (Bartlett, 1983). Thus, science seeks monocrop rather than diversity, universe rather than multiverse. By contrast, social constructionists value diversity and an awareness of a multiverse of perspectives.

For the social constructionist, language is not a device for reporting one's experiences (representationalism); it is a defining framework for those experiences. Thus, a change in language equals a change in the experience. For example, if the effort to make English the official language in the United States were successful, the experience of people of different cultures within the society inevitably would be transformed. The categories and linguistic structures provided by English would provide the final word about what is really "real." Such a move would be akin to making the dominant social experience the politically and psychologically correct experience for all people within the society.

Social constructionists have become particularly critical of such a phenomenon in the mental health field. They believe that the DSM-IV defines the official language, or the politically and psychologically (as well as economically) correct way, for mental health professionals to think and talk about people and their problems. And given this language, mental health professionals socialize their clients into experiencing their lives and their situations through the lenses of the categories the DSM-IV uses to describe them. Further, social constructionists contend that these categories have become part of a larger social discourse, variations of which emerge in the local discourses that choreograph personal relationships. Indeed, they have noted that all human science disciplines in the modernist tradition "characterize, classify, specialize; they distribute along a scale, around a norm, hierarchize individuals in relation to one another, and if necessary disqualify and invalidate" (White & Epston, 1990, p. 74). As we previously described the process,

> People are objectified, and their rich personal experiences and personal stories are subjected/repressed/denied in favor of the normative classification schemes offered as the way they are supposed to experience themselves in order to be members of Western societies. In essence, people internalize and take on the identity of the "objective" category(ies) set forth and validated by human science professionals. (Becvar & Becvar, 1996, p. 282)

This transformation of experience becomes important for clients in therapy who use the language of the DSM-IV to describe themselves and others in their lives. Indeed, diagnostic discourses have become a "part of popular culture and the lay public's own narratives"

(Laird, 1995, p. 153) as people have been socialized to take on the identity of the label or metaphor assigned to them. Having been socialized into a faith in technology and science, people give great credence to a diagnosis that is made using "objective," "valid," scientific instruments. And diagnosis, which by definition is observation in search of deficit, can be made only by "experts" who have been socialized appropriately to work within the language of the DSM-IV. However, a problem emerges when the language is reified, or used as an interpretation of "what is really going on," and the client defines himherself in terms of the problem, saying, for example, "I am schizophrenic" (self/schizophrenic); "I am a manic-depressive" (self/manic-depressive); "I am a delinquent" (self/delinquent).

What is more, other people in the client's life also tend to internalize the deficit label or category and the related explanation and may begin to relate to the client in a manner that brings forth and maintains the reality of the label or category. Thus, discourses, or conversations, logically consistent with the meaning and story associated with a label or category are likely to give rise to and maintain the label or category. As Hoffman (1993) described this phenomenon, rather than the system creating the problem, which is a fundamental assumption of first-order cybernetics, the problem, which exists in language, creates the system. If system members keep talking about the problem, they will maintain the problem. And if they have internalized the concept or construct, they will continue to have and attempt to solve the problem described by the label or category. That is, "The dilemma is that the normative story set forth by professionals in the human sciences is presented as the true story, which represents direct knowledge of the world, or the way things and people really are. And representation of a story as true precludes the search for alternative stories" (Becvar & Becvar, 1996, p. 304).

In other words, people do not relate to other people, they relate to others in a way that is logically consistent with the labels, or metaphors, assigned to them. For example, if "depression" is a part of the language system, and people relate to a person in a way that is logically consistent with that metaphor (typically with attempts to "cheer up" the other), they will participate in bringing forth and maintaining the "reality" described by the metaphor "depression." Indeed, people born and raised in a culture built on the modernist philosophical tradition, such as that in the United States, typically find it difficult to entertain the possibility that an experience to which the metaphor "depression" might be assigned could be anything else. It is real. And they typically find it incomprehensible that people in other cultures who do not have "depression" as a part of their language system can have a different experience and participate in different local discourses. However, Gergen (1994, p. 414) posed an apt question: "How is it that people in other cultures and preceding centuries manage(d) without such a concept, yet contemporary psychologists detect depression in all corners of society (now even in infants)?"

A frequent question social constructionists hear is, "But isn't it [the condition we are seeing] really depression?" For the social constructionist, many answers to this question are possible, including, "It isn't *really* anything," or "It is if you have that concept or construct in your language system." As an analogy, there is the story of the baseball player who turned to the umpire and questioned whether the last pitch was really a ball or a strike. As the story goes, the umpire said, "It isn't anything until I call it something, and whatever I call it, that's what it is." To the social constructionist, it is what it is called, and it stays that way unless it is called something else, but there are many other things it could be called. There are multiple possibilities in a multiverse.

For the social constructionist, reality cannot be experienced directly. The reality experienced is inseparable from the prepackaged thoughts of the society, or what McNamee and Gergen (1992, p. 1) referred to as "forestructures of understanding." Laird (1995, p. 151) noted, "We force our current experiences and perceptions into our prior categories for knowing and thus create what it is we think we see and know." Knowledge, when thought of as narratives embedded in cultural stories, is never final and is always negotiable.

However, empiricist science tends to blind people to the hidden values implicit in the research questions they or others select and to the power relations that exist between superordinate and subordinate groups of society. In effect, empiricist science creates the illusion that everyone lives in a real reality rather than in narratives consistent with the worldview of the society. Figure 2.1 presents some of the basic ideas (or stories or values) characteristic of Western ideologies.

Consistent with the modernist tradition, empiricist science purports to screen out values and to create value-free knowledge. Doing so is essential for maintaining what social constructionists call the illusion of objectivity. Mental health practitioners, for example, are

Representationalism of a
determinate relationship
between words and world
Utopian notions
Ultrasolutions
The work ethic
Individual autonomy
Responsibility and freedom to
"be spontaneous"
paradoxes
Correct/true perceptions
Unilateral control
Survival of the fittest/
competition
Fall and Redemption theology
Either-or dichotomous
thinking
People versus nature
Faith in science and
technology
Separation of mind/body/
social context
Billiard ball causality
Objective, value-free
knowledge
Mental health and illness
Functional and dysfunctional
families

Certainty and uncertainty
Normative psychology
Problems independent of
values
Male dominant gender roles
Racial and ethnic superiority
and inferiority
Separation of self and other
Appearance-reality
Subject/object dualism
Failure as a moral weakness
Valuing rationality
Devaluing emotionality
Science as discovery of real
reality
Observation without
intrusion
The concept of progress
Singular, unified self
Humans as higher-order
creatures in the universe
Belief in essences and
universal truths
independent of culture
"Primitive" cultures as
inferior
Female victim roles
Codependency

*Figure 2.1*

*Partial Listing of the Ecology of Ideas Representative
of Western Ideologies*

expected to use scientific principles in their work and to assess the
outcomes of their work in measurable, quantifiable ways. To the social constructionist, however, knowledge is inevitably value-laden, and
these values are reflected in language and conversation. Further, because all knowledge and thus all therapeutic conversations are value-

laden, social constructionist mental health practitioners attempt to be explicit, or transparent, about values and focus on them as a part of the therapeutic conversation. Further, facts and values are understood not only as inseparable but also as political.

Social constructionist family therapists Anderson and Goolishian (1988, 1992) take the position that a problem is that which a group of people have decided to call a problem. And that which is called a problem is value-relative. Indeed, Dell (1983) suggested that practitioners do not treat problems, they treat values. Further, the group that defines a problem also locates a "cause" or "blame" consistent with the diagnostic discourses of the medical tradition. Thus, in traditional mental health practice, cause and blame are viewed locally, or are attributed to individuals (or couples or families from a first-order cybernetics perspective) rather than being viewed as problems rooted in the ecology of the ideas of the society. Rarely, if ever, are cause or blame attributed to "poverty, racism, sexism or other social experiences that might shape individual experiences" (Laird, 1995, p. 153). For none of these are part of the diagnostic language system.

In essence, to the social constructionist, the individual, couple, or family is not the client. Although individuals, couples, and families may present for therapy, the unit of analysis involves those other people who are "in language" or are "languaging" about the problem, for they participate in creating and help to maintain the problem. Thus, the appropriate unit of analysis in therapy, for the social constructionist, is the narrative according to which meaning is experienced. Meaning, according to this perspective, is not implicit in an experience; rather, people have problems as a function of the way an experience is languaged, or interpreted, classified, or categorized.

For the social constructionist, the therapy conversation, therefore, should not involve discourses about the problem, for engaging in such discourses would be to join those who are "in language" or "languaging" about the problem and would thus help maintain it. That is, attempted solutions to a problem that involve conversations about the problem always stay within the options that are logical to the problem as defined. Moreover, such discussions create the illusion that the problem is "real" rather than being metaphoric or real only relative to a specific language.

The social constructionist perspective does not deny the reality of problems such as poverty, violence, and emotional pain. However,

*reframe*

the focus of therapy is the creation of new narratives or stories about particular experiences, thus allowing clients to escape the logic of a language within which the range of possible alternatives is restricted. To explain, for clients who live their lives according to the "border-line" story or the "bipolar" story, conversations about their lives within those stories tend to keep them anchored in the stories. By contrast, conversations about "exceptions" (de Shazer, 1991), "unique outcomes" (White & Epston, 1990), or strengths allow clients to escape the deficit lifestyle of the DSM-IV diagnostic story. *Solution-focused*

More than 20 years ago, Bateson (in Brand, 1974, p. 25) lamented, "Oh, the damage that's been done to psychiatric thinking by the clinical bias. The clinical bias being that there are good things and there are bad things. The bad things necessarily have causes. This is not so true of good things." As Bateson alluded, most counseling and therapy practice is based on a search for the causes of the bad things, with therapists asking such questions as, "What caused you to drink last Saturday?" In contrast, social constructionists take the position that a more useful conversation is one that searches for the causes of good things. They would ask, for example, "How did you manage to stay sober on Friday?" Such a focus can help the client to deconstruct the totalizing experience of a diagnostic category. Social constructionists assume that nothing is always or never, and that no phenomenon exists to the same degree all of the time.

In social constructionist thought, by viewing truth as relative and science as reflecting political and ideological influences, therapists become aware of many alternative explanations for experiences and behaviors. Thus, social constructionist thinking also challenges another revered idea in traditional mental health practice, the concept of a unified, integrated sense of self that transcends contexts. To the social constructionist, the concept of multiple selves, or "multiphrenia," reflects the different relationships in which people are involved and the different discourses that occur in those relationships (Gergen, 1991). In effect, the concept of the autonomous individual self-destructs and gives way to the concept of the individual experiencing many selves. As Gergen stated (p. 16), "We come to be aware that each truth about ourselves is a construction of the moment, true only for a given time and within certain relationships." Gergen added, "One ceases to believe in a self independent of relations in which he or she is embedded" (p. 17).

A related perspective that fits for the social constructionist is that "bad" experiences can have some "good" consequences and that some "good" experiences can have some negative consequences, as illustrated in the following story of the Chinese farmer (Watts, 1968):

> One day his horse ran away.
> And the neighbors gathered in the evening and said, "That's too bad."
> He said, "Maybe."
> The next day the horse came back and brought with it seven wild horses.
> The neighbors said, "Aren't you lucky."
> He said, "Maybe."
> The next day his son grappled with one of these wild horses and tried to break it in, and he got thrown and broke his leg.
> And the neighbors said, "Oh, that's too bad that your son broke his leg."
> He said, "Maybe."
> The next day three conscription officers came around gathering young men for the army, and they rejected his son because he had a broken leg.
> The neighbors said, "Isn't that great, your son got out."
> He said, "Maybe."

Watts's (1968) point is that no one can know in advance in which direction progress lies. Similarly, from a social constructionist perspective, the meaning of an experience emerges as a function of the narrative describing the experience. Further, for the social constructionist, progress does not lie in the language of deficit and disability that is characteristic of traditional mental health practice whether the client is an individual, a couple, a family, or a larger social system.

Social constructionism concerns epistemology, and as such it is partly metatheory, or a theory about theories. Thus, the process of therapy cannot be neatly designed and categorized. However, therapists who operate according to a social constructionist perspective tend to follow the lead of Foucault. That is, they take the position that social science professionals and mental health practitioners are to be "explicitly committed to critiquing the status quo and building a more just society" and the focus is on developing "empowering approaches to generating knowledge" (Lather, 1986, p. 258).

We end this chapter by acknowledging a conceptual paradox. That is, to say that knowledge is a social construction is to say that knowledge is all made up. This belief, of course describes a "naive solipsism," but it is no more limited than a "naive realism," which suggests that knowledge is all real and assumes that there is a "direct correspondence between an event occurring outside of us and our inner experience of it" (Keeney, 1983, p. 2). However, by offering a logical system that suggests that knowledge is all made up, social constructionism is caught in a self-referential paradox that no logical system can avoid. For it must include itself in its own assertion. Thus, the idea that knowledge is all made up must include the idea that the idea that it is all made up also is made up.

# *Part Two*

# Applications

*I*n Part Two of this book, we take the frameworks described in Part One and apply them to group work. More specifically, we present ways in which a group leader might think about doing group work in a manner that is consistent with first-order cybernetics, second-order cybernetics, constructivism, and social constructionism and discuss some practical ideas for working with groups in this manner. In the discussion in this chapter, we differentiate "group counseling" and "counseling in groups." Our distinction parallels that made by Blocher (1987), who wrote,

> Here we can point to two somewhat different approaches to group counseling. Counselors can either "counsel in groups" or engage in "group counseling." In the first instance, a particular approach to counseling, such as cognitive re-structuring or behavioral approaches, is delivered in a group setting. The primary sources of gain here are viewed as emanating largely from the content of the material discussed, the format within which discussions are held, and the direct intervention of the group leader....
>
> In the case of "group counseling" group dynamics or interactions are the primary sources of gain. The benefit is expected to arise inevitably from the social interactions of the group as it begins to function optimally. In this approach the group counselor functions differently than in the more traditional role of teacher or discussion leader described earlier. Here the group counselor is a facilitator who focuses on process and utilizes the dynamics involved in group interaction, literally to create a powerful social learning experience within the group itself. (pp. 252–253)

This distinction, we feel, is very important. According to our interpretation, Blocher marked a difference between developmental and preventive group work (therapy in a group) and group therapy. Both group therapy and therapy in groups as defined by Blocher are consistent with some first-order cybernetics approaches. However, as we shall explain, group therapy as defined by Blocher is inconsistent with second-order cybernetics as well as with social constructionism. At the same time, we believe second-order cybernetics and social constructionism frameworks can be adapted to fit doing therapy in a group and doing one-to-one therapy in a group context.

In Chapter 3, we discuss the "group" as a construction and explore how one would think about group membership and identity; different kinds of groups; group content and process; group size, structure, and composition; stages of group development; and group leadership from the perspectives of first-order cybernetics, second-order cybernetics, and social constructionism. In Chapter 4, we review the basic principles of first-order cybernetics and discuss ways of thinking about group work from this perspective. We also explicate and present a number of techniques from the Mental Research Institute (MRI) model. In Chapter 5, we present the first-order cybernetics, family therapy models of Virginia Satir and Murray Bowen. In Chapter 6, we revisit the basic concepts of second-order cybernetics, constructivism, and social constructionism and consider ways a group leader in search of a fit with these perspectives might think about group work. We note how group therapy as defined here by Blocher (1987) does not fit with these perspectives, but we also examine techniques from these approaches that might apply to therapy in groups or to one-to-one therapy in groups. Chapter 7 is a summary chapter that includes discussions of a variety of issues. In particular, we focus on epistemological, ethical, and evaluation issues in the practice of group work from the perspectives of first- and second-order cybernetics, constructivism, and social constructionism.

# 3

## Issues in
## Group Dynamics
## and Group Work

*W*e begin this chapter with a discussion of the concept, or construct, of "group" and the construction of knowledge about group dynamics based on this concept. We then explore, from the perspectives of first- and second-order cybernetics, constructivism, and social constructionism, group membership and identity; group therapy; the distinctions between content and process in a group and between individual and group goals; the risks and advantages of group work; group structure, size, and composition; the stages of group development; and finally, group leadership. Whereas some of these issues are the same across the currently existing literature on group dynamics and group work, other issues emerge only when group dynamics and group work are viewed from the perspectives considered herein.

## On the Concept "Group"

Luft (1984) provided a rich sample of questions that drive inquiry and knowledge creation about groups, group dynamics, and group work. Such questions include:

> What is a group? Is the concept "group" needed? Is group behavior the precise sum of the behavior of individuals? Are groups real, or are they

magical or mystical notions? Are there principles or laws governing group behavior? If not, does there seem to be sufficient regularity or order to suggest predictability and pattern?

Why do people form groups? How are groups controlled? What happens to individuals within groups? Why do groups have such difficulty making decisions? Do groups develop like plants or animals? Do groups have illnesses or pathologies? Are there such things as sick groups? Healthy groups? Productive groups? If so, what makes for differences in groups? Can groups help people with psychological problems? If so, how? Can groups be harmful or dangerous to people? If so, how and when? Are groups accountable and responsible? Who is in charge of groups? Are group leaders born, or are they made? Do people behave differently in a group than when they are alone? Why are group activities often so clumsy and complicated?

Can people learn to function better in groups? Do groups brainwash individuals who join them? Are groups instruments for conformity? With respect to the quality and quantity of work produced, are organized groups superior to the same number of persons working individually? (Luft, 1984, pp. 1–2)

The literature on group dynamics and group work provides partial answers to some of the questions Luft asked. Granted, answers to questions tend to generate more questions in a never-ending process. Nevertheless, all questions about group dynamics and group work require as a starting point belief in the concept "group."

As Flemons (1991, p. 1) noted, "Any act of knowing, any knowing act, begins with the drawing of a distinction, with the noting of a difference. A boundary is distinguished from a part of itself.... Knowing is composed of boundaries imposed." Thus, it is by choosing to punctuate a particular configuration of people by the label "group" that the concept "group" is created. And once the concept of group is created, groups are seen and understood through the creation of other constructs for describing their dynamics.

Such constructions become the "stuff" of the minds of professional group workers, and as social constructionists would assert, they also become the "stuff" of the minds of consumers of their professional literature. Thus, to the social constructionist, no book about group work (or any other discipline or subdiscipline) provides descriptions of "real" things "out there." As we wrote elsewhere,

We create theories to order our reality, to explain ourselves, to make sense out of an enormous body of information. In the process, however, we tend to reify our creations. Thus we forget that it is we who have invented the concepts, and that these order-givers do not represent truth in any absolute way. We treat them as real and as the way it is. (Becvar & Becvar, 1996, pp. 306–307)

If the concept "group," and thus the related literature on group dynamics, is constructed, then it also can be deconstructed and reconstructed for heuristic purposes. Further, one cannot speak of group dynamics as a unitary concept. Indeed, a variety of models and related stories for understanding group dynamics have been constructed. Relative to group work in general, theoretical models include person-centered, Gestalt, rational-emotive, transactional analysis, behavioral, reality therapy, and psychodynamic. For symptom-focused treatment in the context of a group, models include those for substance abuse, academic achievement, and interpersonal development, to name a few. Other models for understanding group dynamics include those focused on growth, development, self-help, and support. These constructions are not arbitrary; they were created for specific purposes consistent with the theoretical allegiances of various professionals, the perceived "needs" or problems of a particular population of people, or both. Accordingly, each model has spawned its own related literature on group dynamics, goals, and processes, with the content shifting as a function of the orientation of any one group worker.

# About Groups, Group Membership, and Identity

Many "natural" groups, such as the family, exist that serve species-survival purposes. Other groups are formed with conscious, specific purposes in mind. Sometimes such groups evolve as part of a natural process of sharing the same life space; performing tasks that require, or are more easily performed as, a collective; encountering similar challenges; and dealing with survival issues. Some groups have short lives: when the purpose for which they came together has been accomplished, they dissipate or formally dissolve. Other groups exist for many years, transforming or adding to their original purposes. Some groups continue to exist even when members can describe no practical purpose for their existence. Indeed, it seems that one cannot not be in a group, the largest of which might be the community of people that coexist on Earth. Moreover, people often belong to many groups without conscious awareness of their membership.

One can think of groups in a manner suggested by Bateson (1972). From his perspective, the very act of knowing involves making or creating distinctions and calling attention to a difference. In making distinctions and calling attention to differences people form in their minds clusters or groups of similar and dissimilar things. Thus, in thinking about themselves and others, people place themselves in groups such as male or female, educated or uneducated, child or adult. Although these are not groups in the formal sense, the ecology of ideas composed of the distinctions people make form the different groups by which people think about themselves.

Further, the groups to which people conceptually belong become the bases for their identities. Thus, when people describe themselves they typically invoke membership in groups: woman, wife, mother, teacher, reader, and so forth. Each such identity statement places one in a specific group or category, while also defining such complementary groups or categories as man, husband, father, student, writer, or women who are not wives, are not mothers, are nonteachers, are nonreaders. Accordingly, each group or category becomes the identity member (Watzlawick, Weakland, & Fisch, 1974) for its complementary group or category. An identity member is a logical complement to a metaphor for a category. "High" is an identity member for "low" and vice versa. And these categories or conceptual groupings become the basis for the way people think about themselves, others, and their relationships.

In people's attempts to know, they create distinctions between the groups they see and in which they participate based on the categories they have invented, giving them such different names as school, gang, business, and neighborhood. However, the distinctions they make often reflect value perspectives or biases. So, in one sense, groups are "natural." In another sense, groups are constructions and membership in groups reflects the categories people create in their attempts to "know," define, and describe the groups.

According to Luft (1984), each member of a therapy group inevitably belongs to a network of people whose norms, values, and roles accompany him or her to the group. In addition, stories are socially constructed, which are internalized by members of a society about each "natural" group to which he or she belongs. Thus, there are generic, cultural stories about "women," "teachers," and "mothers" as well as stories about women who are teachers and mothers. For, as described earlier, creating a label for a category of people or things creates membership in the group to which the label refers. What is more, U.S. society has programmed its members with many such labels, or metaphors and stories, which are the "stuff" through which understanding and communication become possible. To illustrate, we invite you to read each of the following metaphors aloud and then to listen internally for the story that gets activated in you when you say the name of each category:

| | |
|---|---|
| Adolescent | Single-parent mother |
| African-American | WASP |
| Senior citizen | Professional athlete |
| Widower | Alcoholic |
| Attorney | Gay |
| Bipolar individual | Victim of child abuse |
| Woman | Soldier |
| Delinquent | Underachiever |

The name for a category and group membership are not identical. However, when a person includes the metaphor of a category in his or her personal identity, the metaphor implies membership in the group of people identified by the metaphor. Further, the person may use such metaphors in conversations about him- or herself.

Our guess is that membership in any group evokes in the group member a story relative to that particular category. We would like to point out, however, that we do not consider such a process of forming categories and hence invoking group membership as either good or bad. Rather, the process constitutes one story about how people consciously know, understand, and communicate. As group leaders think about the people who participate in groups for the purposes of therapy, they may find it useful to be aware of their various identities based both on different categories or conceptual groupings and on the stories the members bring with them. To reiterate, each category or conceptual grouping carries with it stories people tell themselves about themselves and others as well as the stories the group leader tells him- or herself about the members of the group.

The relationship between membership in "natural" groups, group members' stories, and their identities becomes important in group work because group members bring many such identities and culture tales with them, including constructions about normal and abnormal, healthy and sick, and functional and dysfunctional. Further, such categories become the basis for different diagnostic groupings as well as for the process of diagnosis itself. All traditional mental health practice depends for its existence on the belief in these asset and liability categories. They describe the ways people are supposed to be and not supposed to be as well as the things to be concerned about if people are not what they are supposed to be.

Thus, people who present for group work may have been assigned, or may have assigned to themselves, a metaphor that places them in a particular diagnostic category. Indeed, this metaphor may be the dominant story in the life of a group member, and its deficit focus may be choreographing the individual's behavior. It also is likely that the metaphor will influence the behavior and attitudes the individual brings to the group as well as his or her interpretation of the behavior and stories of other group members.

# About Group Work

For purposes of examining the cybernetic, constructivist, and social constructionist perspectives with regard to group work, we have conceptualized three different kinds of groups based on the goals for the group experiences: developmental, preventive, and remedial groups. In this section we discuss each of these types of groups relative to its fit with first-order cybernetics, second-order cybernetics, constructivism, and social constructionism.

## *Developmental and Preventive Group Work*

We use the term developmental group to describe group experiences that have a developmental, or growth, orientation in some valued direction consistent with a given conceptual model. This type of group seeks to provide learning experiences that will foster "effective" human development. Developmental groups might, for example, focus on developmental stage or task theories (such as that of Eric Erickson), effective communication, or parenting. Groups designed to prevent problems (primary prevention) are akin to developmental groups in our thinking. Their purpose is to provide learning experiences designed to preclude the development of problems in the future.

Developmental and preventive groups are logically consistent with the perspective of first-order cybernetics. Both types of groups would be inconsistent, however, with the perspectives of second-order cybernetics, constructivism, and social constructionism. That is, for the group leader to think about and create a learning experience that promotes a specific way people should be is to participate in the creation of a problem. As participant-observers, group leaders would cocreate with the client the problem in need of solution as they ask questions and edit selected pieces of the client's story based on a specific theory that they reflect back to the client. They cannot be objective observers outside the client system; they are one with the client.

The social constructionist views both developmental and preventive group work in a similar manner, believing that to create an expectation that people's lives should take a specific form relative to some valued way of being is to create problems. For example, to have people self-consciously evaluate themselves and others with regard to whether they have accomplished a particular developmental task creates the experience of a problem if they judge themselves, or are judged, to have fallen short in any way. Indeed, developmental and preventive groups cannot not create problems.

In other words, to think in "language" selected ways of being, living, doing, parenting, marriaging, familying, and so forth, reflects attempts at social engineering in the sense of the modernist philosophical tradition. Such attempts promote the notion of a universe, or of a specific and psychologically, politically, and socially correct way to be, rather than the notion of a multiverse, according to which there are many equally useful ways to be. Mental health professionals working from the modernist tradition, therefore, may be understood as agents of the society. That is, they work within the ecology of the ideas of the society and attempt to solve or to preclude problems that are defined by society, focusing on and creating a "vocabulary of human deficit" (Gergen, 1991, p. 14) in a process Gergen described as follows:

> The spiraling of human deficit terminology can be attributed to the "scientizing" of human behavior characteristic of the modern era. As psychiatrists and psychologists try to explain undesirable behavior they generate a technical vocabulary of deficit. This language is slowly disseminated to the public at large, so that they too can become conscious of mental-health issues. As people acquire the vocabulary, they

also come to see self and others in these terms.... And, as the profession is asked for answers to life problems, it is pressed into developing a still more differentiated and expanded vocabulary. (pp. 14–15)

Such a process is consistent with first-order cybernetics, with the observer being separate from and independent of the observed perspective. In other words, developmental and preventive work makes sense if problems are viewed as existing in the society independent of the professional's participation in their creation as he or she works in that society. As Sarason (1981, p. 26) noted, "Psychologists, like most other people, do not see themselves *in* society but rather see themselves *and* society." We would say that they see themselves as observers who are independent of the society and who work to treat problems that evolved independent of their participation. However, any attempts to preclude problems necessarily involve creating a frame of reference that defines classes of behavior or experiences as problematic. As Watts (1972, p. 64) noted: "Other people teach us who we are. Their attitudes to us are the mirror in which we learn to see ourselves.... Our most private thoughts are not our own. For we think in terms of languages and images which we did not invent, but which were given to us by our society.... Society is our extended mind and body."

By contrast, from the perspectives of second-order cybernetics, constructivism, and social constructionism, the problems people experience in their lives are problems only if they are defined as such by the ecology of ideas of a given society. Hence, the idea of developmental and preventive groups is problematic. In addition, from these perspectives, their use represents a form of colonialism (Gergen, 1991). For to promote a preferred way to be according to some generic theory or model, or similarly to attempt to preclude a way of being that is construed as problematic, is to fail to respect the uniqueness of different gender, ethnic, cultural, and racial groups.

Leading a prevention group presumes knowledge of the etiology of the problems that the group experience would preclude. From the perspectives of second-order cybernetics, constructivism, and social constructionism, however, problems exist only as they are created in value-based conceptual models. To speak of cause in a linear sense is to be inconsistent, and to define such causes is to assume that one can "know" with greater certainty than in fact is possible. Thus, from these perspectives, thinking and languaging about the possibility of a problem give it an existence. Such activities also promote related discourses as well as the belief that the problem and related discourses are things about which people should be concerned. Indeed, group conversations may include a focus on concern about people who are not concerned about the possibility of a problem.

## Remedial Group Work

We define a remedial group as one that is convened for the purpose of dealing with an existing "problem." We call this type of therapy a form of symptom-focused treatment (Becvar & Becvar, 1996). Remedial, or symptom-focused, groups work with such issues as substance abuse, child abuse, delinquency, adult children of..., academic achievement, and divorce.

Second-order cyberneticians, constructivists, and social constructionists have fewer problems with remedial group work than they do with group work focused on development or prevention. However, their remediation would not involve treating the metaphor assigned to the problem behavior. In addition, they would consider the metaphor "remedial" as problematic, for remediation implies correcting errors or faults that are assigned to a person rather than to the context (Caplan & Nelson, 1973). Accordingly, it is the person's deficits and deficiencies that are to be corrected. Attempts to treat the metaphor thus serve to participate in the creation and maintenance of the reality of the problem. Similarly, attempts to remediate the person participate in the creation and maintenance of the idea that the locus of responsibility for the problem resides with the person. In other words, treatment of a person relative to a metaphor assigned to a symptom or class of behavior tends to reify the problem and related solution as well as the locus of responsibility for having the problem.

Indeed, from the perspectives of second-order cyberneticians, constructivists, and social constructionists, success can seduce professionals into reifying constructions. For example, if a student is labeled an underachiever and the story is told that he is an underachiever because he has low self-esteem, he may be encouraged to participate in a growth group or remedial group designed to foster greater self-esteem. If his achievement subsequently improves, a reasonable assumption is that the story about his low self-esteem was correct. However, from our perspective, any one of a number of experiences, including events in the client's life about which the therapist is unaware, may have influenced the outcome. Again, "'Working' is not an epistemological notion" (Longino, 1990, p. 93). A social constructionist would suggest that in the situation just presented, the therapist celebrate the client's success but not reify the connection between underachievement and self-esteem.

For second-order cyberneticians, constructivists and social constructionists, remedial group work would not involve discourses about the problem. Rather, because they would assume the problem and related story to be social constructions, they would assume that they can be deconstructed or that a new story can be constructed. That is, frameworks can be expanded. Stories about other parts of a client's life that have not been told or have not been considered to be worth telling can be recounted. In Chapter 5, we explicate specific approaches to group work that are consistent with second-order cybernetics, constructivism, and social constructionism.

# Content and Process, Individual and Group Goals

Group interaction can be described as having two aspects, content and process. We define content as the issues or concerns presented within the group by group members. Content thus refers to what group members talk about relative to the task or the purpose of the group. We define process as how group members relate to one another. Process aspects of a group have to do with the different roles played by those in the group or the interpersonal dynamics between group members and between the leader and group members. Process in this sense describes the way in which group atmosphere is created as members and leader help each person attain influence and recognition as well as feel valued and accepted. Optimally, it describes the interpersonal interactions that create psychological safety and allow members to feel free to express themselves and to help one another accomplish their personal goals. Process thus has been referred to as encompassing the general goals for each therapy group.

Content and process have also been used to refer to two different kinds of goals for the group experience, those that we refer to as individual and group goals. That is, each group member has a content goal relative to his or her search for solutions to a particular problem. In addition, to facilitate the achievement of individual goals, group goals are established, or evolve, such as achieving a sense of coherence and fostering group trust. Accordingly, such group process goals also become individual goals. From first- and second-order cybernetic as well as constructivist and social constructionist perspectives, the goals of any therapy experience should be the goals of the individual members of the group. When an individual member of a group has achieved that for which he or she joined the group, it is appropriate that the experience end for that person.

However, group process goals also become individual goals. That is, every group evolves a normative way for the members to be with one another that is assumed to facilitate the achievement of goals by individual members. These process goals may involve basic ways of communicating effectively and building relationships. They also may address group members' "needs" for affiliation, nurturance, acceptance, and recognition. Some "general goals [for group members] shared by most counseling groups in most settings with most populations" have been described as follows (Corey, 1995, pp. 7–8):

- To learn how to trust oneself and others
- To foster self-knowledge and the development of a unique sense of identity
- To recognize the commonalty of the participants' needs and problems
- To increase self-acceptance, self-confidence, and self-respect in order to achieve a new view of oneself
- To find alternative ways of dealing with normal developmental problems and of resolving certain conflicts
- To increase self-direction, autonomy, and responsibility toward self and others
- To become aware of one's choices and to make choices wisely
- To make specific plans for changing certain behaviors and to commit oneself to following through with these plans
- To learn more effective social skills
- To become more sensitive to the needs and feelings of others
- To learn how to confront others with care, concern, honesty, and directness
- To move away from merely meeting others' expectations and to learn to live by one's own expectations
- To clarify one's values and decide whether and how to modify them

In the context of Western society and its related ideology, such goals feel "right," rather like parenthood, apple pie, and Chevrolet. Accordingly, they constitute some of the unquestioned assumptions on which many models of group work are based. However, these process goals constitute a culture-bound idea of what every person should know, be, and do. They thus represent values, and implied in those values are self-assessment and judgment by others as to whether or not one has achieved the goals. Those who believe that group members should decide specific goals for themselves must remain aware that general goals like those set forth by Corey (1995) become the hidden agenda of the group, or the values implicit in the group process.

Further, therapists who "facilitate" the group process with these general goals in mind are socializing participants into the values implied in the goals. They also may be participating in the creation of "misfits" in the context of group members' racially, culturally, and ethnically different natural networks. Such behavior not only affects the group members but indirectly deprecates the dynamics and interpersonal processes of those natural groups.

From the perspectives of second-order cybernetics, constructivism, and social constructionism, perhaps the most important process goal facilitated by the leader is that of helping participants learn to communicate about how they communicate. This goal, which we describe as "learning how to learn," also may help group members develop "an epistemology that has a conscious awareness of itself" (Keeney, 1983). Indeed, second-order cybernetic, constructivist, and social constructionist perspectives are not value-free when it comes to the goals implicit in group work. That is, leaders operating in a manner consistent with these perspectives may well promote some of the values and goals listed above. In addition, the values and process goals implicit in their perspectives also include the following:

- Participants are a part of a totally interconnected universe
- How other people interact with an individual is relative to how the individual interacts with them, and vice versa
- The sense of self one experiences is context-relative—that is, it is relative to the context or relationships of which one is a part; each individual has a "self" that is composed of many selves

- Participants are living their lives in the stories of the dominant culture and many of these stories are focused on deficits
- The story one tells oneself about oneself, or about another person, is but one of any number of stories that may fit equally well if not better, and no such story is "true"

All groups promote conformity to the norms of the group as reflected in the group dynamics facilitated by the leader. Indeed, groups cannot do otherwise, for these specific dynamics are implicit in the concept "group." Process goals typically are decided (directly or indirectly) by the group leader, and thus they reflect his or her theoretical orientation.

In the light of this discussion, two important questions come to mind. First, how in a context of conformity can a group leader promote respect for each group member as a unique emotional system? And second, how can a group leader involve members in decisions about the group process to be facilitated? We will provide some answers to these questions when we discuss specific approaches to group work from the perspectives of second-order cybernetics, constructivism, and social constructionism in Chapter 5. For now, we turn to a consideration of the advantages and risks associated with group work.

# Advantages and Risks of Group Work

From different vantage points one can see advantages and risks for almost any human experience, and certainly group work provides no exception. Some of the risks in group work are associated with the social power of the group. Some are associated with models in which high levels of expressed emotion are expected of group members. Some are associated with the unique configuration of the group members who constitute a particular group. Some are associated with leaders whose theoretical orientations to group work are described as no pain, no gain. Some are associated with the structured ambiguity of classical laboratory groups in which the leader leads by not leading. Outcome studies indicate that although the mean scores of counseled groups and control groups show no difference, there is greater variability within the counseled groups than the control groups (Bergin, 1963; Blocher & Biggs, 1983; Hartley, Roback, & Abramovitz, 1976; McDevitt, 1987).

From such findings, one can conclude that anything that is potentially therapeutic can also be toxic.

At a pragmatic level, group work may be an economical way for agencies to deliver services when resources are limited. Similarly, for professionals in private practice, more income can be generated from group work than from seeing individuals, couples, or families. These viewpoints may be considered advantages to group work. From the perspective of the conceptual frameworks of interest in this book, however, one must take a broader perspective when weighing the advantages and risks of group work.

That is, in addition, focusing on the specific goals of individual members, the group experience may provide a context for meeting such human "needs" as affiliation, nurturance, acceptance, and recognition. However, a social constructionist would have a problem with the concept of "need," which has been defined as "1. a requirement, necessary duty or obligation; 2. a lack of something deemed necessary" (*Webster's Collegiate Dictionary,* 1995). Defining any metaphors as "needs" cannot help but create an experience of self-evaluation and deficit.

Further, as worthwhile as providing affiliation, nurturance, and so forth, may seem, as the group experience meets such needs, members' awareness may be heightened regarding the extent to which these needs are not being met in their natural contexts. In other words, meeting these needs in the group context can create more serious problems for members in the natural settings in which they live and work. At the very least, members will learn to view their relationships in their natural settings through different lenses. And, as mentioned earlier, they may become "misfits" in these settings, they may attempt to change others in their natural settings, or both. From Haley's (1976) cybernetic perspective, from an ethical standpoint the therapist must be concerned not only about his or her work with clients but also about how any changes that occur in the clients will affect other people in their lives.

Indeed, the group can be viewed as a miniature society that can facilitate the transfer of learning to natural settings by providing a context for trying out new insights, attitudes, and behaviors. Thus, the group may be viewed as a laboratory for experimenting with alternative ways of being, feeling, thinking, and behaving. Again, however, the dilemma that arises is that group members may seek to colonize people in their natural contexts into their new and supposedly wonderful ways.

However wonderful the new ways of being may seem in the laboratory setting, they cannot not affect other relationships that are important in the lives of the members. Stated differently, each group member lives within a network of relationships characterized by redundant, predictable ways of relating. If new behavior, regardless of its merits, is attempted in these relationships, it will likely cause confusion for the others. Although these others may adapt, it is more likely that they will attempt to return things to the way they were. Indeed, the transfer of a group member's learning about interpersonal skills from the group to the natural setting may have less to do with the efforts of the group member than with the receptivity of others in the natural setting to the possibilities for better relationships or with a lack of sensitivity on the part of the group leader regarding how change in a group member's behavior may affect the natural setting.

# Group Structure, Size, and Composition

From the postmodernist perspective, the most effective physical structure for a group, selected from the models described by Leavitt (1951), would be the circle rather than either the "Y," the chain, or the wheel. Consistent with first-order cybernetics, second-order cybernetics, constructivism, and social constructionism, the circle allows members direct access to one another and facilitates awareness of patterns of interaction among members. In the spirit of King Arthur and Camelot, the circle also suggests equality of status and thus has particular relevance for second-order cyberneticians, constructivists, and social constructionists, who place value on the "nonexpert" stance of the leader.

In general, as group size increases, several dynamics, which are not independent of one another, seem to occur. First, the relative frequency of and opportunity for participation by all group members tends to be reduced (Castore, 1962; Shepherd, 1964). Second, psychological involvement on the part of some members may decrease. Third, the probability is greater for one or two members to take more dominant roles. Fourth, the leader's ability to monitor the effects of the group experience on individual members may be reduced. Fifth, members may experience less cohesiveness and satisfaction (Munich & Astrachan, 1983). We would lean toward six to eight members as the optimal group size. Groups of that size have been shown to have a higher probability for active participation than larger or smaller groups (Hansen, Warner, & Smith, 1980).

Group composition is a much more difficult topic to address for the simple reason that the number of variables to consider is infinite. Who is in a group does make a difference. For example, if a group leader opts for homogeneity and compatibility, he or she reduces the amount of diversity in the group. Our view is that difference and diversity are important resources. At the same time, we realize that too much diversity may undermine the ability of the group to work together to achieve its goals.

One also may make decisions about group composition based on the roles of the members and the functions that accrue to these roles, for in any system or group roles tend to evolve. Thus, each group can be viewed as people performing roles that complement one another and that serve to maintain the group. However, people who aspire to preconceived roles may or may not find their choice of role respected. Thus, we believe that selecting members on the basis of the roles and functions that need to be performed is probably an empty exercise.

Also with regard to group composition, leaders must deal with the question of how much is too much or too little relative to specific characteristics, such as skills, ideas, resources, goals, attitudes, and values. A related question is, how do we know who has how much of what? Another important question concerns the leadership style of the group leader and his or her choice of model. What kinds of people fit which group leader?

Sometimes clients can make better judgments than the group leader about whether a group experience is appropriate for them. As stated earlier, it is important that the group leader relay to potential members the purpose of the group, the process to be facilitated, the process goals of the group, and the theoretical model to be utilized. In addition, he or she can help prospective group members decide if the group will be appropriate for them by asking questions such as the following:

What is your story about your experienced need for therapy?
What is your story about the problem, need, or dilemma?

Who in your life has told you that you have a problem in need of solution?

What is the story of your seeking therapy at this time?

What is your story about your coming to see me about group therapy?

What is your story about selecting group therapy rather than an alternative?

If you have a successful group experience, how will you be different?

What is your story about what the group experience will be like?

Who in your life would be most pleased if you were to accomplish your purpose in coming to group therapy?

Who would be most disappointed if you were to change?

What are your expectations for this group experience?

What would you like to know that would help you decide about whether this group experience will be appropriate for you?

From my description of what the group experience may be like and what would be expected of you, what fits for you and what does not fit for you?

Can you afford to attend the group in terms of time and cost?

Still another question that comes to mind about group composition is whether group members should share the same symptom metaphor and experience a common symptom-focused treatment (e.g., alcoholism, adult children of..., delinquency, underachievement). From the perspectives of first- and second-order cybernetics, constructivism, and social constructionism there is no theoretical reason why clients with different symptom metaphors cannot be mixed. Indeed, one could conceive of advantages for mixing metaphors in terms of increasing diversity and the variety of resources in the group.

A similar issue is whether one should mix people of different ages and sexes, or people of different races, ethnic groups, and cultures, in a group. One could create lists of advantages and disadvantages for almost any combination of variables. But for any group, one cannot know which of the distinctions created may make a difference. From the second-order cybernetics and social constructionist perspectives, conscious attempts to try to control the variables to create a group composition that will minimize risks and maximize success may participate in creating the very phenomena such efforts seek to preclude. Being concerned creates concern.

# Stages of Group Development

Many models for the stages of group development have been developed (Bion, 1961; Braaten, 1974; Dunphy, 1974; La Coursiere, 1974, 1980; Tuckman, 1965; Yalom, 1975; Zurcher, 1969). Each of them represents the vision of its developer and concerns both the theory used in the group and the purposes of the group. Thus, the notion of "stage" in group work serves as a heuristic construct or a conceptual ladder to help the therapist organize his or her thoughts about group process. From a second-order cybernetic perspective, conceptualizing stages of group development creates a reality. Instead, the group should be allowed to evolve. The models that are consistent with the other postmodern perspectives, particularly those consistent with social constructionism, attempt to avoid what McNamee and Gergen (1992, p. 1) referred to as "forestructures of understanding." In the following paragraphs, stages that seem to fit group development from the perspective of first-order cybernetics are discussed.

*Planning Stage.* In this stage, which occurs prior to the beginning of actual group meetings, many initial questions regarding the group's overall purpose are addressed. The group leader establishes the structural, procedural, and compositional elements of the group by setting forth how the group initially will be organized and who will participate.

*Orientation Stage.* This stage begins with the initial meeting of group members and is characterized by formal or informal orientation as well as exploration of the group's overall purpose and objectives.

*Organization Stage.* In this stage, the group members come to terms with how the stated purpose of the group complements or conflicts with their individual goals and agendas. Each member discusses the relative usefulness of the group to him or her, and the purpose of the group is modified, as appropriate, so that it best meets the needs of the participants.

*Process or Work Stage.* In this stage, there is an increased level of cohesion and a shared sense of purpose among the group members. Each member of the group is able to engage in activities and tasks that fit the purpose of the group as defined by the needs of the individual members.

*Termination Stage*. Because all therapy groups are finite and individual participation will end at some point, this stage provides activities for the transition of members to life without the group.

No model describes discrete stages with clean boundaries. From our perspective, it is useful to view a group as a dynamic system in a continual state of renewal and change as it organizes around its stated purpose. The group should be allowed to evolve.

# Group Leadership

One cannot think about the concept "group" without thinking about leadership. As Gardner (1990, p. 80) noted, "Leadership [in any arena] is necessarily concerned with group behavior." However, for the concept of leadership to be meaningful, it must be considered in context. That is, from a cybernetic point of view, one cannot speak meaningfully about a leader without also considering its logical complement, the follower(s). Leaders and followers are conceptually and functionally connected.

However, leadership behavior does not necessarily create follower behavior, and vice versa. Indeed, natural groups may form without formal leadership, although even in those situations it is likely that a leader will soon be designated or will evolve. Many people may aspire to be leaders, but whether they are successful in becoming leaders depends upon group members' ascribing that role to them. Leaders and followers maintain one another in their complementary roles and continue to exist in the relationship as long as the purposes of the group are being achieved.

One also cannot speak meaningfully about group leadership without designating the kinds of groups involved. Just as different kinds of groups require specific leadership styles, leaders following specific models for group work must adhere to specific leadership styles to remain consistent with those models. One may also speculate that therapy groups at different stages of development or facing particular challenges require different leadership styles.

Although it is possible to discuss leaders in terms of their assigned or institutional authority (e.g., department chairs, supervisors), assigned or institutional authority does not translate into effective leadership unless people are willing to follow. Not surprisingly, attempts by institutional authorities to require people to follow a designated leader fail more often than they succeed.

The success of a therapy group is closely associated with the effectiveness of the leader. For therapy in general and group work in particular, the kind of leadership required is relationship authority, which we define as a person's behavior, attitude, and ways of being that influence others to accept and work with that person. Some relationship authority may accrue to people who help followers experience the following effects set forth by Carkhuff (1969) as the preferred conditions for a helping relationship: empathy, respect, concreteness, genuineness and self-disclosure, confrontation, and immediacy. Relationship authority evolves when group members experience support, caring, and structure appropriate to the accomplishment of both individual and process goals. Paradoxically, the rendering of such support, caring, and structure can also be seen as skills that influence people to accept authority and render them amenable to influence. Abrogating authority may be the most powerful form of authority.

The term "facilitates" is closely associated with leader behavior in group work. This metaphor feels and is generally accepted as benign, but it can also be viewed as an insidious form of social control (Becvar & Becvar, in press). That is, it is hard to "resist" group process that is "facilitated." Indeed, the accepting and nurturing environment that group leaders foster has a power of its own. Aware of this power, second-order cyberneticians, constructivists, and social constructionists attempt to build a more egalitarian relationship by being "transparent" about both the values implicit in the process that will be facilitated and their expectations regarding group members' participation in that process.

There is a paradox, however, implicit in the concept of being transparent about process values and goals. This transparency, or openness, about agendas can also be viewed as being very controlling. In the field of family therapy, second-order cybernetic, constructivist, and social constructionist approaches that seek to bring to life the concept of participant-observer, transparency, and openness about the process of the therapy have been viewed as insidious forms of manipulation that give the therapist power as a result of denying the power of the facilitative conditions. Golann (1988a, p. 56) wrote, "Power obscured eventually emerges—a therapeutic wolf clad as second-order sheep." This issue is not unlike the one that arose in the 1950s and 1960s relative to the "nondirective" approach of Carl Rogers.

Finally, one cannot speak meaningfully about group leadership without addressing its legal and professional contexts. As a mental health professional, the group leader has responsibility for ethical, procedural, and administrative aspects of the group. The responsibilities associated with group facilitation are based on the ethical and legal imperatives promulgated by various laws and codes of ethical conduct. The specific day-to-day responsibilities of a mental health professional may vary according to jurisdiction and political climate, but the basic ethical responsibilities remain constant and all ethical codes are derived from the philosophical concept of beneficence.

The concept of beneficence, which serves as a primary moral imperative for the helping professions, dates back at least 2,500 years to the time of Hippocrates in classical Greece and holds that it is the duty of the helper to engage in acts of kindness and, in the process, to do no harm (Eliot, 1910). Today, standards of ethical and legal conduct exist, in some form, in every human society. In Western cultures as well as others, beneficence is a basic expectation that society holds for those who engage in therapeutic roles. This expectation exists regardless of the particular theoretical orientation of the therapist.

With regard to therapy, societal standards go beyond the mere admonition to "help and do no harm." Society defines the practice of therapy and sets the standards that define who may do what to whom as well as the parameters in which "it" may be done. Indeed, these parameters define the breadth and scope of mental health functioning and practice. Such parameters for professional practice provided by society are congruent with the professional practice of first-order cyberneticians. However, second-order cyberneticians and social constructionists would add other dimensions to the responsibilities of the group therapist. For them, the therapist also is responsible for the following:

- Discerning a "need" or "problem" (developmental, preventive, or remedial) that may be met in a group context
- Deciding that the group context is a better context within which to meet that need than are other experiences

- Accepting an assignment to conduct a therapy group to meet the need
- Selecting members for the group, informing members of the advantages and risks involved in their participation, selecting the theoretical model to guide therapeutic discourse in the group, selecting the process goals that will be facilitated, and creating the physical and time context for the group experience
- Creating perhaps more serious problems by attempting to meet the need that defines the purpose of the group

In addition, the group leader is responsible for:

- The effects of any change the group members may make on other people in their natural contexts
- The goodness of fit of the theoretical model selected and of the process goals for all group members, including women and members who are ethnically, racially, or culturally diverse
- The possible reification of the metaphor defining the symptom-focused treatment that may be the focus of the group

We are aware that there are many other aspects of group work that we might have addressed in this chapter, and we are also aware that those included could have been discussed in more depth. For the purposes of this book, however, our rather brief review seemed appropriate.

# 4

# First-Order Cybernetics and Group Work

*I*n the first part of this chapter we review some basic principles for thinking about clients, problems, and counseling that are consistent with first-order cybernetics. In the second part of the chapter we consider the approach to individual and family therapy of the Mental Research Institute in Palo Alto, California (MRI), which reflects a first-order cybernetic perspective. As a part of this discussion we describe our view about ways in which certain concepts and methods of this approach might play out in group work.

## Basic Principles of First-Order Cybernetics

Mental health practice from a first-order cybernetic perspective is consistent with the modernist philosophical tradition. From this perspective it is assumed that (a) people's sensory perceptions provide them with a view of reality; (b) certainty is possible, and thus the objective reality "out there" is absolute and can be discovered; and (c) phenomena can be observed without changing them in the process. Assumptions about therapy include the ideas that (a) the "problem" exists as a real thing in itself; (b) as a real thing, the problem can be treated; and (c) change can be predicted and orchestrated by someone outside the system. In other words, first-order cybernetics is the world of discovery through observation, and in this world assessment, diagnosis, and treatment are understood as primary functions.

What particularly distinguishes the family therapy approaches of first-order cyberneticians from the approach of other traditional mental health perspectives in the modernist tradition is the shift in the unit of analysis from the individual to the system. First-order cybernetics may best be characterized as the "interactional view." That is, rather than examining the characteristics of individuals, first-order cyberneticians focus on the patterns of interaction between persons, on an analysis of people in context.

Accordingly, first-order cyberneticians are less concerned than traditional mental health practitioners with what is going on inside the person exhibiting problem behavior. Instead, they look to the intimate and immediate social network and to the larger social network of which the immediate social network is a part. They assume, as Amatea & Sherrard (1994, p. 11) stated, that "when components (i.e., people, families, neighborhoods, specific subcultural groups) demonstrate problems, it is because they have not been sufficiently socialized as to their proper role and structure by the hierarchical layer immediately above the layer demonstrating deviance." The therapeutic task for therapists therefore is to ascertain the structural defect in the system(s) of which the individual is a member (diagnosis); formulate an intervention strategy; and repair the defect in the structure of the system(s) of which the individual is a part.

The following principles elaborate on the basic ideas that constitute the ways of thinking about clients and the process of change from a first-order cybernetic perspective. We acknowledge that some of these ideas could also fit second-order cybernetics, constructivism, and social constructionism.

*Principle 1.* Behavior labeled as either problematic (mad or bad) or nonproblematic (sane or good) is "normal," or a part of the natural ecology in the context of a given relationship.

*Principle 2.* If the behavior of a client makes sense in context, the presenting problem is viewed as a symptom of a disturbed relationship. Similarly, when relationships are viewed in context, the therapist sees normalcy of the "disturbed" relationship in the context of the larger system.

*Principle 3.* The therapist understands as somehow logical a unique response of a particular client and thus normalizes it rather than measuring the appropriateness or inappropriateness of the behavior or experience relative to some normative standard.

*Principle 4.* Implicit in every theory of therapy is a set of values or ideas about how one is supposed to be, do, feel, and think and how one is not supposed to be, do, feel, and think. No theories are value-neutral. All theories of therapy are conscious designs for producing behavior, attitudes, beliefs, and feelings consistent with a specific set of values. Without a set of values, there are no problems in need of solution.

*Principle 5.* People are not simply the way they are independent of context (that is, substantively); they are the way they are as a function of a given context (that is, their behaviors are contextually relative). People are not simply specific kinds or types of persons; they are the way they are with others as a function of the way others are with them. Each is a part of the context of the other.

*Principle 6.* The system is its own best explanation. The system is what it is and does what it does.

*Principle 7.* In attempts to understand a system, the focus is on current behavior.

*Principle 8.* One cannot understand individuals out of context because people always exist in some context. That to which people necessarily belong has no outside for them.

*Principle 9.* Each client who presents for therapy lives within a natural network of relationships with others. These others relate to the client in a way that is logically consistent with the metaphors their society has assigned to the classes of behavior under which the client has been categorized. Behaving with the client in a way that is logically consistent with the metaphor assigned to a class of behavior maintains or escalates the behavior. Consider the case of an adolescent who has been categorized as delinquent. When enough people, including parents, the school principal, counselors, the court, and so forth, tell the same story about the delinquent and behave in a way logically consistent with the metaphor "delinquent," the story associated with the metaphor soon becomes the story the adolescent uses to describe himself or herself.

*Principle 10.* People define their identity, or sense of self, relative to the context of the relationships of which they are a part. Thus, there is no unified singular sense of self. Instead, each person has multiple selves that he or she experiences in the context of different relationships.

*Principle 11.* No person "causes" the identity of another. The client and each other person in his or her network make up a system in which each serves as the identity member for the other. For example, "rotten kid" and "mean teacher" define and maintain the identity of the other.

*Principle 12.* A person's identity is closely tied to the relationships in his or her life. One's experience of the person he or she is, is contextually relative. When a first-order cybernetician is asked, "What kind of a person is Kevin?" the appropriate response would be, "I don't know what kind of person Kevin is. I only know how he is with me when I am the way I am with him. And I can only tell you my story about Kevin, and my story says more about me than it does about Kevin." Further, the response to the question, "What kind of person are you?" can only be answered relative to context: "At a baseball game I am _____." "At church I am _____." "After a trying day at work I am _____."

*Principle 13.* Change occurs as a function of a change in context:

$$\text{Change in context} = \text{Change}$$

If the context within which a behavior occurs remains the same, it is likely that the behavior will continue or will escalate.

*Principle 14.* A change in context in a relationship can lead to a change in the behavior of one or both people in the relationship.

*Principle 15.* A change in context in a relationship can also lead to a change in the meaning one assigns to a behavior or an experience. Context is not an objective thing out there. That is, people do not live in a real context. Rather, they live in their construction of the out there that they create.

*Principle 16.* When attempting to solve problems, people often commit the "environmental fallacy" (Churchman, 1979). That is, each problem has a context or an environment in which it is intricately embedded. That context or environment is far more difficult to perceive than the problem as punctuated by society. When one fails to perceive the context of a problem, however, and invokes solutions that do not address it, he or she is committing the "environmental fallacy" and is participating in the creation of higher-order problems.

*Principle 17.* If symptomatic behavior makes sense in context, it may reflect a certain "wisdom" in the client's life. It is important to respect this wisdom and to help the client to develop an expanded vision of the changes he or she proposes to make.

*Principle 18.* No one can do just one thing. Any change in a client's behavior inevitably affects his or her relationships with others.

*Principle 19.* If people would like others to be different with them, they must see themselves in the context of the relationship and see that they have been participating in creating with the other the behavior they would like to see change.

*Principle 20.* When contexts change and the new context is maintained, the behavior of people in a relationship changes. Likewise, when the behavior of one person in a relationship changes and this new behavior is maintained, the behavior of the other person in the relationship cannot stay the same.

*Principle 21.* Attempts by one person to change the behavior of another person while not changing his or her behavior will not only not change that behavior but will maintain and perhaps participate in the escalation of the focal behavior. Attempts at unilateral change in that which is bilateral will fail.

*Principle 22.* No behavior can maintain itself on its own energy; it needs a logical complement.

*Principle 23.* Acting in a way that is illogical or different will break the redundant, reciprocal pattern of a relationship.

This set of general principles provides a framework for thinking about and developing models and specific interventions for therapy as well as for group work. As we noted elsewhere,

> The rule regarding change from a systems perspective is differentness. A change in behavior requires a behavior that is not logical in that context. Thus there is no prescribed form that therapy must take, nor should there be. The basic limitation for acceptable therapist behavior is not exceeding the bounds of ethical practice. (Becvar & Becvar, 1996, p. 84).

Indeed, first-order cybernetics is not a pragmatic theory. It probably is best viewed as the skeleton of a theory that has been fleshed out in a variety of ways in the field of family therapy. While the pragmatics of therapy can be drawn from these family therapy models, they also can be gleaned from the great variety of models for working with individuals. However, for one to do so, the latter must be translated into a cybernetic framework. Indeed, first-order cybernetics is a way of thinking about people and change.

# The Interactional Theory of the Mental Research Institute

In this section we describe the first-order cybernetic approach to family therapy developed and used by the team of researchers and therapists at the Mental Research Institute in Palo Alto, California (MRI). In the next section, we show how this approach might be applied to group work. Because we do not believe that the MRI approach provides a particularly good fit with group work, we have taken the liberty of constructing a fit while at the same time being careful to be reasonably consistent and respectful of the basic tenets of the model.

In many ways the interactional approach of the MRI is seminal to most systemically oriented therapies (Fisch, Weakland, & Segal, 1982; Watzlawick, Beavin, & Jackson, 1967; Watzlawick, Weakland, & Fisch, 1974). Gregory Bateson, Richard Fisch, Jay Haley, Don Jackson, Virginia Satir, Paul Watzlawick, and John Weakland all contributed to the development of this pragmatic, brief therapy approach to understanding people and their problems. In a manner that is consistent with second-order cybernetics, the inevitability of the influence of the therapist is acknowledged, but the general flavor of the approach is that of first-order cybernetics in that the observer considers himself or herself as outside the system and as someone whose inputs from outside are required to change the system.

In this approach, the therapist focuses on observable behavior in the relationships between people. Dysfunctional behavior is viewed as being maintained inadvertently by the people in a relationship in their interpersonal contexts. The therapist focuses on the present context in which problems occur and the nature of current relationships rather than looking to the past or attempting to understand how things got to be the way they are. Regardless of how problem behavior started, the therapist assumes that problems are maintained by the ongoing behavior of the client and others in his or her interpersonal context. Thus, problem behavior is considered to be normal or a logical role in that context.

From this perspective, therapy involves a process of understanding how problems are maintained and then, using this understanding, designing a plan for interrupting the interactional sequence of which the problem behavior is a part. The therapist assumes that the client is doing the best he or she can in his or her current interpersonal context and that the problematic behavior can be changed or the problem resolved as a function of changes in context, including changes in the meaning the client has assigned to the problem.

The MRI approach is nonnormative in that it is not attached to societal standards regarding the way individuals, marriages, or families should be to be considered "healthy" or "normal." For example, from this perspective, grief in the context of the death of a loved one makes sense and the length or intensity of the grief experience is understood as personal to the client, not to be compared to the length or intensity of grief experienced and defined as normal by the general population. Indeed, the process of applying normative standards is viewed as participating in the creation of problems. Rather, as stated in Fisch, et al. (1982, p. 127), "The purpose of brief therapy is to influence the client in such a way that his original complaint is resolved to *his satisfaction*" (emphasis added). As a nonnormative approach, the MRI stance would not fit either developmental or preventive group work.

A great emphasis is placed on a client's ability to change problem-maintaining behavior. That is, the client is assumed to have the resources, strengths, or abilities to effect necessary changes in his or her relationships. Because behavior change requires a change in context, change must occur in how people in the client's interpersonal context relate to one another. As they begin to act in ways that are illogical to the problem-maintaining behavior, the behavior will change. Another way to describe a change in context is a change in the meaning attached to a behavior as sufficient for change, or a prelude to change, occurs.

The MRI approach is complaint-based. Clients present with concerns about themselves or other people in their lives and therapy is terminated when the clients no longer have the complaint. If another complaint is presented after the resolution of the first complaint, it is treated as a new problem in need of solution. This approach has been used to treat a wide range of common, everyday individual, marriage, and family problems as well as acute and chronic problems, such as anxiety, depression, eating disorders, school and work difficulties, and schizophrenia. Treatment is defined as successful when a client has completely or significantly achieved the specific behavior changes he or she has agreed upon with the therapist.

The pragmatic focus of the MRI approach has been described as a four-step procedure (Watzlawick, 1978):

1. Develop a definition of the problem in clear and concrete terms.
2. Investigate all solutions to the problem previously attempted.
3. Define the change to be achieved in clear and concrete terms.
4. Formulate and implement a strategy for change.

According to the MRI model, there are two kinds of changes, first-order and second-order. These two types of changes can be illustrated by discussion of the nine-dot problem presented in Figure 4.1. The nine-dot problem instructs you to connect all nine dots with four straight lines without lifting your pencil from the paper. We invite you to try it now.

An almost universal assumption that people make when attempting to solve this problem is that in searching for a solution, they must stay within the boundaries of the square formed by the nine dots. Such attempts are defined as attempts at first-order change.

In the four-step sequence of the MRI approach, steps one and two seek information about the definition of the problem and about previously attempted, logical, first-order changes. In other words, answers to steps one and two provide information about the conceptual and interpersonal nine-dot box in which clients are living their lives. When the logical solutions to the complaint, which are attempted within the confines of the box, do not solve the complaint, solutions outside the interpersonal and conceptual box may be required. That is, one may need to change one's assumptions and view the dot pattern as a non-square, allowing the pencil to be moved outside the conceptual box and the problem to be solved. Rather than a change within the system, there is a change of the system. Indeed, "second-order change has been compared to a leap of imagination experienced in moments of creativity. It requires a response that is illogical to context, paradoxical, or crazy when considered within the framework of existing rules" (Becvar & Becvar, 1996, p. 98). The solution to the nine-dot problem, presented in Figure 4.2, illustrates the idea of breaking out of the box into a new realm of meaning.

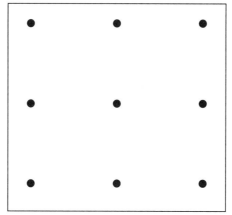

## *Figure 4.1*

### *Nine-Dot Problem*

Answers to the questions posed in steps one and two of the four-step MRI procedure are important, for they provide information about the client's frame of reference as well as the solutions he or she has attempted that are logically consistent from within that frame. Fisch, et al. (1982) noted five ways in which clients typically attempt to solve problems:

> (1) attempting to force something which can only occur spontaneously; (2) attempting to master a feared event by postponing it; (3) attempting to reach accord through opposition; (4) attempting to obtain compliance through voluntarism; and (5) conforming to the accuser's suspicions by attempting to defend oneself. (p. 128)

In their view, the problems people bring to therapists generally have been maintained by one of these five attempted solutions. Accordingly, they have described five major classes of interventions that parallel these five attempted solutions. We discuss their intervention classes in the next section. However, for now it is important to note that, from the MRI perspective, all interventions are planned and are created to interrupt the attempted solution. That is, the therapist cannot not intervene. Further, interventions are designed with a focus on "interdicting the problem-maintaining behavior of the client or others, or in appropriate cases, by altering the client's view of the problem so

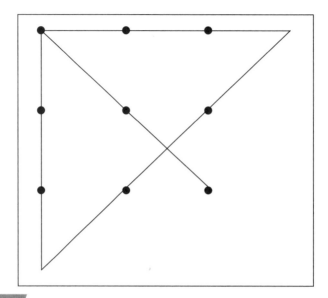

*Figure 4.2*

*Solution to Nine-Dot Problem*

that he no longer feels distressed and in need of further treatment" (Fisch et al., 1982, p. 127).

Another important aspect of the MRI approach is the concept of reframing (Watzlawick, Weakland, & Fisch, 1974). According to this concept, a situation or problem is shifted from its old context, or frame of reference, to a new context. To explain further:

> The process involved here is the creation of reality as we perceive/define it. This means that we categorize objects and events into classes of action with particular meanings. Once we assign an object or event to such a class, it is extremely difficult to see it belonging to another class, and thus as having a different meaning. Reframing, on the other hand, changes the class of the object or event. (Becvar & Becvar, 1996, p. 103)

Reframing by a therapist may be an important prelude to requesting a change in behavior. However, the reframe must be believable and acceptable to the client and also must fit the situation as well as, if not better than, the current frame with which the client has defined the problem and has attempted first-order solutions. Thus, a thorough understanding of the client's existing frame of reference, acquired through steps one and two of the approach, is necessary before an alternative frame can be suggested. What is more, when selecting an alternate frame, its utility is more important than its truth. As a problem is moved to a different context of meaning, new answers and behavior alternatives become possible, and thus a second-order change is effected. As stated by Efran and Lukens (1985):

> The form of a problem—the domain in which it exists—determines the form of its "cure." The phrasing of a question establishes the kinds of answers that can be formulated. When "reframing" proves effective, it may be because the domain in which the problem occurs has shifted, and new answers become available and acceptable. (p. 28)

Although paradoxical interventions are often associated with the MRI approach, in actuality they do not often appear in the practice of the therapy. Indeed, Fisch, et al. (1982, pp. 127–128) wrote, "In our own view the use of paradoxes as interventions is relatively rare; the term is attributed too loosely and casually to any intervention which strikes traditional therapists as novel, ironic, or contrary to 'common sense.'"

What often are viewed as paradoxical interventions are not paradoxes from the MRI perspective. Such interventions are examples of second-order change, for they redefine or change the meaning of a situation and open up new behavior alternatives. An example of such a "paradoxical" intervention is prescribing the symptom. It is logical to attempt to cheer up a depressed person or to try to help the person get rid of his or her depression (an attempted first-order change). However, since feelings are not subject to conscious control—for example, through willpower—such attempts to alleviate the depression are likely to fail, and after they fail the depressed person may become more depressed about not being able to rise above his or her depression. The attempted solution is an example of "attempting to force something that can only occur spontaneously." Thus, it is not the original depression that is the problem, it is the depression about the depression that is the problem.

Although suggesting that the person hold on to the depression (second-order change) would be illogical from the original frame of reference, this suggestion may solve the problem of the person being depressed about his or her depression. Reframing the depression as important to the person, noting that any attempt to get rid of the depression prematurely may cost him or her the opportunity to learn something from the depression, is quite logical from another perspective, or frame. Thus, the paradoxical intervention ceases to be paradoxical or illogical, for it is only illogical and paradoxical relative to the original frame of reference. Prescribing the symptom becomes a logical solution from the alternate frame of reference, within which it is a first-order change. In essence, if an intervention consists of a meaningful reframe, the concept of a paradoxical injunction is deconstructed.

Whereas a client's definition of a problem and descriptions of previously attempted solutions will provide information about the client's existing frame of reference, his or her responses to the therapist's questions about the changes to be achieved (step three of the MRI approach) will help to elicit a clear and concrete vision of the desired future state. Although clients tend to be very articulate about what they do not like and about the problem they wish to eliminate, they tend not to be very articulate about what their lives would be like if they were the way they wanted them to be. Focusing on the desired future state, therefore, may be a useful activity in that a first step to acquiring a new behavior pattern may be to imagine oneself doing it. In one's imagination, one can break into the realm of new possibilities. By contrast, a person cannot pursue that which he or she cannot even imagine. On its own, the desire to eliminate a problem will not provide this vision.

# Applying the MRI Model to Group Work

Although there is certainly much more to the MRI model than we have discussed, the general principles we have described provide enough of a sense of the model for us to now move to a discussion of how these ideas might translate into group work. Because it is a first-order cybernetics model, many of the usual concerns related to group size, group structure, and group composition fit when applying the MRI approach. Note also that a typical MRI contract for number of therapy sessions specifies 10 or fewer, and the four-step procedure for problem solution could be construed as fitting four stages of group development.

As a first-order cybernetician, the group leader would provide leadership with regard to the process and problem-solving method to be utilized in the group. He or she would be a strategist and a designer of interventions. Further, given that the approach is pragmatic, with a problem-solving orientation, group process and the utilization of the resources of group members would be facilitated to this end. Although the group might be formed around symptom-focused metaphors, there is no theoretical reason why symptom-focused metaphors could not be mixed.

The group leader also might well move into the pragmatic, problem-solving stance of the MRI approach with a minimum of formal structuring, although he or she could opt to include more such structuring. With regard to formal structuring of the interpersonal process in the group, the following rules would seem to fit the MRI model. The leader might ask group members to:

- Listen respectfully to one another.
- Speak only for themselves.
- Speak to a specific member of the group when participating in a discussion.
- Represent anything said as their own perspective.
- Observe carefully how the person to whom they are directing statements receives them. If their ideas do not appear to fit the person, or if the person states that they do not fit, the group members must be respectful and accepting. What has worked for some group members may not work for others.
- Receive statements, ideas, and suggestions from others in a way that respects their efforts as attempts to be helpful. A group member's only obligation is to hear what the others have to say. No one is required to adopt the suggestions of others.

In the group, minimal attention would be directed to formal relationship-building, although relationship-building would most likely follow from the intense involvement of the leader and his or her interest in helping group members. The group leader would be acutely aware of, and would empathize with, the pain expressed by group members but would not dwell on talking about any problems. Talking about a problem would be understood as a logical, first-order change response that would not solve the problem.

We now discuss each of the steps of the MRI approach as we feel they would apply to group work.

## Step One: Defining the Problem

Following step one of the MRI's four-step procedure, the leader would pose a question that would solicit from each group member his or her definition of the problem in clear and concrete terms. The leader might begin by saying words to the following effect:

> Tell us (me) about your problem.
>
> Let's begin by hearing from each of you about the problem or complaint that brought you to the group.

The leader would then ask questions aimed at eliciting from each client specific, clear, and concrete behavioral definitions of the problem. General and amorphous definitions of the problem such as "Everything is going wrong" or "My life is falling apart" would not be acceptable. This activity may take some time with the first few group members, but from observing others creating concrete definitions, those still to take a turn would learn the "rule" and would become more concise. It is very important at this stage that the group leader not attempt to make preliminary reframes or bridge to step three, attempting to obtain definitions of the change desired.

Group members may hear similarities and differences with their own problems in the problem definitions of others. After each member has taken his or her turn, the group leader might well ask some variation of the following questions to elicit discussion of similarities and differences:

> As you listened to one another, what did you learn about your own situations?
>
> What similarities and differences between you did you infer?

Throughout the whole process of step one questioning, the leader would be gathering information about each group member's frame of reference. Building on an interactional focus in which symptomatic behavior is understood to make sense or fit the interpersonal contexts in which group members live their lives, the group leader would normalize rather than pathologize. That is, he or she would see and hear normalcy in context for that which someone coming from an individual psychology perspective might view as pathological. The leader would assume that each group member has a coherence within his or her frame of reference and that the behavior has a coherence within the group member's network of relationships.

## *Step Two: Eliciting Previously Attempted Solutions*

Step two of the four-step procedure would provide a more detailed perspective on the clients' frames of reference. The focus would be on solutions to the problem that were previously attempted, or on all logical, first-order, attempted solutions. The group members' responses would provide a further glimpse into the box (or set of nine dots) in which the clients live their lives. To our knowledge, this particular activity originated with and is unique to the MRI approach. The following, or variations on the following, question might be asked:

What have you tried to do to solve your problem?

The problem may be drinking, not getting along with a spouse, problems in school, stealing, drug use, lack of control of one's children, and so forth. As with step one, the leader would ask detailed questions seeking clear and concrete articulation of all attempted, unsuccessful solutions to the problem. A related question that also could provide a glimpse into the frame of the client is a variation on the following:

What solutions have you thought about but have not yet attempted?

In a continuation of step two, the leader might ask questions about the relationship of others in the clients' interpersonal networks with the clients' problems and attempted solutions. Such questions might include, for example:

What solutions have other people suggested to you?

What have other people in your life done in their attempts to assist you in solving your problem?

Who are these people?

How would you describe your relationships with them?

Although eliciting this type of information is not specifically articulated as a part of the MRI approach, from a broad interactional perspective such information may prove useful. In addition, the group leader might ask group members to develop interpersonal network maps that include the names and roles of important people in their lives with regard to the issue of the problem. Figure 4.3 illustrates such an interpersonal network map.

Following review of a client's map, the group leader might ask another set of questions that would logically fit an interactional focus. For example:

Who in your network suggests that you have the problem you seek to solve?

If this problem were not an issue for these others, would you be concerned about the problem they say you have?

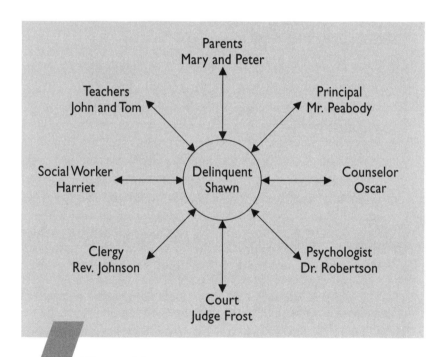

*Figure 4.3*

*Sample Interpersonal Network Map*

If you solved this problem to the satisfaction of those who suggest it is a problem, what other problems might they want you to work on?

If you were to solve this problem, who in your network would be the most pleased and who would be the most disappointed?

After everyone has spoken, the group leader might invite the members to discuss their answers. Such a discussion would be especially important if any of the group members are in the group because others have suggested that they have a problem although they do not believe they do. The discussion might create an awareness of the way in which problems are embedded in interpersonal networks.

The idea offered by Keeney (1983) that any problem is a solution to another problem also might well fit step two, opening up a different set of questions:

What other problem in your life is your present problem solving?

If you were to solve this problem, what other problems might result from this change?

What is the downside to resolving your complaint?

Such questions relate very closely to the idea suggested by Watt's story about the Chinese farmer (presented in Chapter 2), which could be told to the group. In addition, the leader might ask group members to develop and articulate environmental impact statements about the consequences of changing their behavior to help them gain a perspective on the benefits and liabilities of change. An important concept in this regard is the systemic notion that you can't do just one thing. Solving a problem may create other problems and, in some cases, can create more serious problems. Any desired change might affect important relationships in the lives of group members. To convey this concept, the group leader might ask a question such as the following:

If you were to quit drinking (get along better with your spouse, be more successful in school, stop stealing, stop using drugs, get along better with your children, etc.), what relationships might be changed or ended as a consequence of this change?

## *Step Three: Defining the Desired Change*

Step three, defining the desired change in clear, concrete terms, is important for several reasons. First, the clients' statements would become the basis for their knowing when they have achieved the goals of therapy. Recall that the MRI approach takes a nonnormative stance and that the therapist does not judge when goals have been accomplished. That decision is each client's alone. Specific questions a group leader might ask to aid clients in defining the changes they wish to make could be variations on the following:

> If you were to be successful in this group, exactly how would you be different?
>
> What is the smallest change you would need to make to know you had accomplished what you came for?

Follow-up questions by the group leader and discussion by the group members about their answers to those questions might address what Watzlawick, Weakland, and Fisch (1974) referred to as the Utopian Syndrome. The idea underlying the Utopian Syndrome is that people may come to therapy with unrealistic goals based on the idea that a problem-free life is possible as well as desirable. Such a belief creates a never-ending search for utopia. From the MRI perspective, a problem-free life is never possible, for every value frame designates a different set of problems. Thus, the MRI posture is to work to solve only the presenting problem. If other problems come to the fore, they are treated as new problems to be solved. Attempts to resolve issues and problems once and for all are utopian and are doomed to fail. Nevertheless, by helping a group member articulate his or her desired future state in specific terms and by facilitating discussion about goals that are attainable, the group leader would greatly enhance the member's probability of success as well as the maintenance of the change.

## *Step Four: Creating Strategies for Change*

Step four involves creating a strategy for change. Perhaps the most important component of the group leader's conceptual repertoire at this stage would be the idea that what the clients are doing is not working and that doing more of the same of what does not work makes no sense. Complementing this awareness would be an understanding of the box, or set of nine dots, that limits the range of options available to each group member. The group leader would have heard the group members' articulations of what they have tried and what has not worked. The leader would also have challenged the goals of group members and limited them to those that are more likely to be obtainable than utopian.

Consistent with the MRI approach, any strategy for change would have to be custom-designed to fit the unique circumstance and situation of each group member. A reframe, if used, therefore would have to be acceptable and believable to the group member at whom it is directed. Similarly, an operant, behavioral assignment for work outside the group would have to be custom-designed for each member as would any "paradoxical" interventions. If a reframe, an operant assignment, or a paradoxical injunction suggested by the group leader happens to fit more than one group member, that situation would be coincidental and not intentional on the part of the leader.

Much of the work in step four would involve respecting the idea that each group member's problem is normal—that is, that it fits his or her interpersonal context as well as his or her frame of reference. This concept is important in that however painful a certain behavior may be, it is familiar and embedded in a network of relationships. It is known and predictable, whereas change describes a future that may seem good from the outside but is not known. That which is not known can be frightening. Thus, the leader must be sensitive to two conflicting messages from clients: "Help me change" and "Don't change me." Such requests are for both change and stability. Clients' previous attempts at first-order change have become a part of the stability of the system. If attempts at second-order change are implemented, the stability of the system may be threatened and the system may attempt to shut down the change that ostensibly is desired. This concept would be especially important if a group member were to present in a state of crisis and request expedient change to relieve pain. If the group leader were to respond to this request for expediency of change and lose sight of the member's unstated request for stability, the attempted change might not be successful. It would be important that both messages be respected. Based on this idea, all group members might be encouraged as follows:

Go slow.

Experiment with your new ideas and ways of being in your relationships and see how they fit.

Hold on to your problem a little longer so that you can learn as much as you can from it.

Discuss the changes you are contemplating with people in your network, and ask them what they think about your ideas before you begin to change.

Each of these statements could be construed as a paradoxical injunction, suggesting restraint from change. However, in the light of the belief in the group member's request for both stability and change, they would make sense. From this alternate frame of reference, they cease to be paradoxical.

From the MRI perspective, a reframe does not necessarily mean rewriting life stories. Indeed, a general principle to which advocates of this approach adhere is the importance of looking for the smallest intervention that may resolve the complaint. A simple twist on a word may constitute an effective reframe. For example, parents who describe their child as impossible might find the concept "challenging" to be a more useful metaphor. A person who describes himself or herself as depressed might also be described as disenchanted, demoralized, or disgusted. And a person who describes himself or herself as shy may find it meaningful to think in terms of cautious or of not having found a relationship in which he or she feels safe.

A reframe also may be a simple assertion, such as the following:

It's easy to be loved when one does loving things.

When one does loving things, one becomes lovable.

Other kids get away with more things than you do. The difference is that they do a sufficient number of things that are expected, and so they don't get watched so closely.

One thing I have noticed about children is that they will get what they need. If it is not given to them, they will find a way to take it, steal it, or perturb people until they get it. What is interesting is that they view getting yelled at as much better than being ignored.

Another type of reframe may involve asking a question that sends the message that the group member participates in how others interact with him or her. Examples are:

> How would you have to be with Joe so that he might be different with you?

> What would you have to do when you go home to upset your parents?

A reframe may directly challenge a group member's self-imposed "be-spontaneous" paradox:

> As I listen to you, I hear you assuming that you have to feel motivated in order to study. In my experience, one can study without feeling motivated to do so. When you study and perhaps learn a little bit, you may find yourself being motivated.

> It would be nice if we had to do only the things that we want to do. Sadly, most of the things demanded of us in life involve doing things that we don't want to do, like getting out of bed in the morning, doing the dishes, cleaning the garage, and doing homework.

A reframe may suggest a desired outcome from completing an operant task:

> One of the exciting things about doing a task that is challenging or difficult is the satisfaction one feels at having met the challenge.

> It is truly fascinating how parents and teachers let up on scrutinizing when one begins to do just a few things that they would find acceptable.

A reframe may focus on a particular aspect of a paradoxical injunction:

> Yes, it might be very hard for you to become a successful student. It might cost you many of your current friends, which would be difficult because you feel you don't really fit in with the other students. How much success do you think you could experience without your current group of friends cutting you off?

I can see how important your problem is to you. As long as you
have your problem, people expect less of you. Of course, the
downside is that you restrict the opportunities available to you.
The decision about whether to get rid of your problem or keep
it is a tough one.

A reframe may involve wondering aloud:

I wonder what would happen if you scheduled times for your child
to have ten tantrums each day.

I wonder what would happen if you joined your child and had a
tantrum with her.

I wonder what would happen if you and your child both took a
time-out when the two of you are getting on each other's nerves.

I wonder how your friends would respond to you if you pretended
not to be depressed.

I wonder what story your wife is telling herself about you, and I
wonder what you are doing that confirms her story about you.
I wonder what you might do differently, what you might do
more or less of, so that her story about you might change.

As mentioned at the outset of this discussion, interventions would
have to be designed to fit the needs of each client. However, our view
of a reframe is that it plants the seed of an alternative way of thinking
not only for the client on whom it is focused, but for other clients as
well. Many of the seeds sown might find fertile ground and thus also
might be meaningful to other group members.

In step four of the MRI approach as it might be carried out in a
group, members could participate in reframing or developing alternate conceptions for one another. A challenge for the group leader
would be to observe and direct the group away from the search for
"whys" on the assumption that knowing why (if it were possible to
know the definitive why) would not necessarily resolve the problem.
Group members could also brainstorm alternative ways of viewing
situations, role-play existing relationships in their own or other group
members' lives, and rehearse alternate, illogical, or second-order-change
ways of being in these relationships that would break the existing,
redundant patterns.

As stated earlier, clients typically attempt to solve problems in
five basic ways as described in Fisch, et al. (1982). At this point, we

present interventions, consistent with the MRI approach, for cutting off those classes of attempted solutions. To reiterate, a basic assumption underlying all MRI interventions is that what clients are now doing is not working. More of the same or its opposite will not work. Second-order solutions will be "different" or illogical from the original frame of reference.

*1. Attempted Solution: Attempting to force something that can only occur spontaneously.* This category of solutions describes problems of bodily functioning or performance, including, among others, sexual performances, tremors and tics, appetite problems, stuttering, insomnia, and obsessions. In the normal course of a life, appetite, sleep patterns, and all of these other bodily and mental performances fluctuate. In most cases, the fluctuations are temporary and often are viewed as such. For most people, the fluctuations correct themselves spontaneously. A problem arises when normal fluctuations are viewed as problems and conscious attempts are made to correct and preclude their recurrence. Such attempts are unrealistic and will fail. When people attempt to consciously control a natural fluctuation, which will pass in its own good time, or when they try too hard, they elevate the fluctuation to problem status.

As inferred by the nine-dot problem, it will not work to encourage the client to stop trying to solve the problem. Efforts at trying to stop trying to solve the problem are in the same class of events (the same set of nine dots) as consciously trying to solve it. A set of strategies that extend outside that nine-dot box and therefore may work include the following:

- Plant the seed that it would be more of an ordeal for the client to have the problem than it would be for him or her to get rid of it. Tell the client, for example, "Since you can't sleep, use the time productively by cleaning the bathroom thoroughly."
- Tell the client that it is important to bring on or to keep the problem for diagnostic purposes.
- Tell the client that the problem must be active as a step for eventually controlling the problem.
- Instruct the client to consciously schedule a time to experience the symptomatic behaviors.
- Tell the client that the complaint is beneficial in some other aspect of his or her life.

- Tell the client to consciously think about and dwell on the problem or to consciously expose himself or herself to situations that encourage succumbing to the problem.

*2. Attempted Solution: Attempting to master a feared event by postponing it.* This category of solutions describes phobias, shyness, writing blocks, or other creative or performance blocks that can arise with or without the "help" of another person. The dilemma with this type of solution is that it is aimed at the goal of absolute mastery, of performance without risk of failure. Of course, everyone experiences natural fluctuations in how well they perform things throughout life. Typically, the person can accomplish a particular task. However, at times, he or she may have some difficulty doing so. If the person dwells upon the performance block, thinking, for example, "What's wrong with me? Other people seem to be able to _____ ," a simple anxiety can reach a phobic level. Avoidance behavior therefore may become the norm. The solution that is usually attempted is to prepare for the feared event in such a way that the event will be mastered in advance. Therapeutic interventions along this line, advocating more of the same, probably will not be successful and may participate in maintaining the problem even when the expert's voice is added to the client's own.

From the MRI perspective, the therapeutic strategy for this class of problems and attempted solutions is to "expose the patient to the feared task while restraining him from successfully competing it" (Fisch et al., 1982). For example:

- Fear of taking exams—"Take the exam but pick out one question that you will leave unanswered."
- Fear of creating an imperfect art project—"Build a flaw or an imperfection into the design of the project."
- Driving phobia—"Explore the dangers of driving while sitting in your parked car. Do not think about the pleasures of driving. Do not drive."

*3. Attempted Solution: Attempting to reach accord through opposition.* This class of solutions involves issues requiring mutual cooperation, such as "conflicts between parents and their rebellious children or teenagers, employee disputes, and problems of grown children with their elderly parents" (Fisch et al., 1982, pp. 139–140). The attempted solution in these cases is that "the complainant demands the other person treat [him or her] as 'one up,' and . . .the demand for 'one-upness' is phrased as being right or being in charge, and [is] pursued by threats, force, or by logical argument" (p. 140). Such first-order solutions are contradictory to achieving the one-up position that is sought.

Illogical, second-order solutions to such problems that involve reframing might include the following:

- Taking a "one-down" position, or a position of weakness, in which one makes requests rather than demands and thus paradoxically attains the one-up position.
- Breaking the escalating, symmetrical pattern by becoming unpredictable or uncharacteristic (different).
- Encouraging responsible behavior by not taking responsibility and not protecting, both of which can be constructively frightening.
- Making specific, but casual, requests rather than demands.

   *4. Attempted Solution: Attempting to attain compliance through requesting voluntarism.* This category of solutions involves what are called "be-spontaneous" paradoxes, that is, requests for behavior that can occur only spontaneously or voluntarily. Examples of such requests include, "I want him to want to do it," "Do what I ask you to do, but do it voluntarily," and "I know what I want him to do, but I don't want to tell him. If I told him and he complies, then he would be doing it because I requested it and not because he wanted to do it." Typically, such attempts to attain compliance involve efforts to be benevolent. However, feelings are not subject to conscious control. Requests for specific behavior can be complied with, whereas requests for specific feelings constitute "be-spontaneous" paradoxes. The latter would not necessarily be a problem if the dilemma involved could be addressed directly, but when such requests appear in the context of marital or parent-child relationships, attempts to address them may be taken as challenging.

   A second-order solution for dealing with a "be-spontaneous" paradox is to get the person involved to ask for what he or she wants directly. The challenge for the therapist is to develop a frame that will make sense to the client and help him or her to make the suggested change. To this end, the therapist could:

- Describe attempts at benevolence as being more destructive than direct requests.
- Explain the "be-spontaneous" paradox, saying, for example, "Behavior is subject to conscious control. Feelings are not. Most things we do are things that we don't want to do. If you ask someone to do something rather than ask that the person enjoy doing that thing, it may get done even though it may not be fun to listen to the griping."

*5. Attempted Solution: Confirming the accuser's suspicions by defending oneself.* This category of solution involves situations in which there is suspicion of some act that is considered to be wrong by both parties, with *A* accusing *B*. *B* denies the accusation and defends himself or herself. Of course, *B*'s defensive behavior confirms *A*'s suspicions inasmuch as *A* subscribes to the belief that if one were innocent, one would not need to defend oneself. Thus, the accuser-defender pattern maintains itself and escalates. This game continues as long as both parties continue to play. One person needs to behave differently. Therefore, the therapist might:

- Suggest that the defender agree with the accusations to the point of absurdity.
- Use an intervention called "jamming," which involves breaking the pattern by changing the game. If the accusation is one of drinking too much, the defender could be instructed to keep careful records of the amount he or she drinks and could also at times pretend to be drunk when he or she is not in order to test the observation powers of the accuser.

In addition to suggesting interventions, making assignments for work outside the group also would be an important part of step four. Such assignments could be operant or paradoxical. They might involve having clients take different roles or having them respond differently in relationships in their natural network. The focus is on breaking the pattern within the relationship or the pattern in the client's relationship with himself or herself.

The MRI approach was designed for work in individual, couple, or family therapy, but we believe that with some modifications it could be utilized effectively in group work. Typically, the approach is strategic, in that the therapist designs reframes and assigns the tasks to be accomplished. Although some of these tasks may well fit more than one member of the group, tailoring interventions to fit each unique client is a hallmark of the approach. The general formula described herein can be considered a conceptual map, but the approach is not formulaic.

Although the MRI approach is nonnormative in terms of the particular form individuals, marriages, and families should take, implicit in the model are some aspects of effective human relationships and communication processes that could be readily translated into group work for enhancing human relationships (in groups). Groups could be formed with an eye to instructing and facilitating group members toward some of these values, much as one might teach the approach to therapists. In this sense, some of the process goals would involve increasing the conscious awareness of group members with regard to some of the basics of human communication, the interactional component of human problems, human experience as perception, simultaneous requests for stability and change, "be-spontaneous" paradoxes, first-order and second-order change, making requests directly, and the five categories of attempted first-order solutions as they relate to solving personal and interpersonal dilemmas. Further, even paradoxical interventions need not always be strategic or without explanation and may be effective if they are fully explained to highly motivated clients.

Would the MRI purist conduct interpersonal training in a group as described in this chapter? Probably not. In our view, however, the basic concepts involved in the MRI approach may be construed as a preferred and normative standard of performance for all relationships. In this sense, there is a second-order cybernetics or participant-observer perspective in the MRI approach. Finally, inasmuch as we have provided here only a rather brief overview, we recommend that therapists undertake more intensive study before attempting to implement the MRI model in group work. The reference list at the end of this book contains several works that may be useful in increasing proficiency in this approach. However, we know of no work that provides a recipe for applying the approach in a group setting.

# 5

## More First-Order Cybernetic Models and Group Work

*T*his chapter builds on the ideas presented in Chapter 4, providing an explanation of the first-order cybernetic models of Virginia Satir and Murray Bowen and a description of how these models could be applied to group work. Satir's model seems to provide a good fit for therapy in groups and for group therapy. Bowen's approach has been utilized in group work with couples, and we extend it here to work with groups of individuals. We acknowledge that we have taken liberties with both models in constructing a fit with group work. We take responsibility for any fit or lack thereof that you may see as we apply concepts from these approaches to groups.

## Virginia Satir's Process Model

Perhaps no model of family therapy lends itself better to the practice of group work with individuals, couples, and families than that of Virginia Satir (1967a, 1967b, 1971, 1972, 1978; Satir & Baldwin, 1983; Satir, Stachowiak, & Taschman, 1977; Simon, 1989). As Satir was a member of the MRI group from 1959 to 1966, she was influenced not only by systems thinking but also by the human potential movement and the work of Carl Rogers and Abraham Maslow. After she left MRI, Satir became director of training at the Esalen Institute, also in California.

As a first-order cybernetic or observed-systems model, Satir's approach, we believe, could be used effectively in developmental, preventive, and remedial group work. Although later in her life Satir was perhaps more identified with what might be termed the human potential movement than she was with family therapy per se, our explication of her approach is presented in terms of its original perspective and applications. Indeed, Satir herself conducted human growth workshops utilizing the basic principles of her family therapy approach.

Satir viewed the family as a rule-governed system that provides the context for constructive or destructive growth and development. She believed that the family was the social system through which the salvation of the world could be accomplished. Her therapy was an extension of herself and her warm, nurturing, genuine, deeply caring interpersonal style. Thus, she brought a strong humanistic, nurturing presence to the field of family therapy. She was the consummate communicator, and in her work she sought to help family members feel loved and valued.

Indeed, in Satir's model of the healthy family, members frequently exchanged loving behavior and openness and honesty were highly valued. In the healthy family, Satir wrote, "anything can be talked about—the disappointments, fears, hurts, angers, criticisms as well as the joys and achievements" (Satir, 1972, p. 14). For Satir, the healthy family was flexible and could solve problems effectively. Its members were open to experience. In line with these beliefs, Satir built her approach to therapy on the following basic assumptions:

All people have a natural inclination toward positive growth and development.

Individuals possess all the required resources for positive growth and development.

In the family and other human relationships, there is mutual influence and shared responsibility. That is, "everyone and everything is impacted by, and impacts, everyone and everything else. Therefore, there can be no blame—only multiple stimuli and multiple effects" (Satir, 1982, p. 13).

Although in therapy the therapist must take the lead in interaction between clients and therapist, each person is and must be in charge of himself or herself. People can effectively be in charge of themselves when they become whole.

Satir described parents and child as the primary survival triad and believed that the child's identity and self-esteem develop in the context of constructive or destructive interactions in this triad. It is important to note, however, that although she felt that the parents were important factors in a child's development, she did not blame them for a child's problem, and in her therapy she did not allow people to dwell in the pain of the past.

Satir also wrote about a second triad, that of body, mind, and feelings. She believed that physical symptoms in different parts of the body were metaphors for and expressions of emotional distress. She, therefore, used sculpting in her therapy to allow clients to experience themselves, their relationships, and their feelings in a safe context and thus to evolve different awarenesses and interpretations. Sculpting involves the therapist or family members arranging themselves in a configuration relative to each other and creating a statue as a symbol of characteristic behavior of each family member.

In addition, Satir (1972) believed humans communicate through five basic communications stances, placating, blaming, super-reasonable, irrelevant, and congruent, that manifest themselves in both body position and verbal behavior. A placater presents as a passive, weak, self-effacing individual who always agrees with others. The blamer usually disagrees with others and always finds fault with them. The super-reasonable person is extremely logical and intellectual and assumes a computer-like rigid posture devoid of feelings. The irrelevant individual's communication is unrelated and distracting to what is happening. This individual considers neither self nor others. The congruent individual sends messages in which words and feelings match, and neither the self nor the context is denied (Becvar & Becvar, 1996).

It was Satir's belief that people cannot not communicate and that messages must be sent and received clearly if individuals are to flourish. Indeed, communication is basic to her perspective. In her therapy, however, she was not eager or anxious about changing people. Rather, she had great confidence in herself and in the capacity of people to respond to the conditions that she felt would promote their wellness and positive self-esteem. Thus, she wrote: "I had developed a profound and unshakable belief that each human can grow.... My search is to learn how to touch it and show it to the persons so that they can use it for themselves. That was, and still remains, the primary goal in my work" (Satir, 1982, p. 16). Indeed, Satir believed that change was inevitable under the right conditions. Accordingly, she wrote:

> Some therapists think people come into therapy not wanting to be changed; I don't think that's true. They don't think they *can* change. Going into some new unfamiliar place is a scary thing. When I first begin to work with someone, I am not interested in changing them. I am interested in finding their rhythms, being able to join with them, helping them go inside to those scary places. Resistance is mainly the fear of going somewhere you have not been. (Simon, 1989, pp. 38–39)

As noted earlier, Satir's therapeutic style reflected her capacity to be caring and accepting. In a caring and receptive environment, she believed, clients would become more open to experience, including their own experienced fears, anxieties, hopes, and dreams. As a therapist, Satir thus modeled effective communication. She was in charge of the therapy but was neither anxious nor impatient for people to change. More specifically, she actively, warmly, acceptingly, and authoritatively:

- Insisted that each person speak for him- or herself
- Clarified communication
- Helped each member feel heard even if he or she spoke what to others was nonsense
- Focused on the here and now and on solutions rather than on complaints about the past
- Pointed out positive intentions
- Demonstrated loving behavior
- Helped people receive loving behavior
- Actively promoted clear and direct communication
- Promoted close proximity and touching
- Showed people how to touch each other tenderly and, in the case of parents touching children, firmly and protectively
- Worked with different combinations of pairs, connecting with each member in loving and caring ways
- Actively sought and asked questions about unexpressed feelings, thus making analog digital
- Cut off topics and conversations that were destructive and demeaning

■ Cut off emotional negative, destructive feedback, elicited direct emotional expression, and suggested positive intentions

Satir believed that the therapist should be constructively spontaneous, experimenting with different behaviors to help people grow. She was flexible about time and space for therapy, often utilizing marathon sessions of several hours in different settings. Her repertoire included sculpting (Simon, 1972; Duhl, Kantor, & Duhl, 1973), games, family chronology, and humor. She used strings and blindfolds to demonstrate the interconnection between family members and how they cannot help but influence one another (Satir & Baldwin, 1983). She provided clients with experiences that illustrated the effects of different ways of being with one another.

# Applying Satir's Model to Group Work

If it were applied to group work, Satir's process model might fit any group of individuals, couples, or families meeting to work on similar or even mixed symptoms. Given the emphasis of this approach on interpersonal dynamics, whatever the presenting problem or the shared metaphor that might bring group members together, the group process would be the healing aspect. The goal would be to have group members learn to work with and learn from one another.

Although we perhaps cannot adequately explain in words the intricacies of Satir's work as a therapist, which was one with the person she was, we can highlight some specific techniques she used that may fit group work with individuals. For example, one of Satir's tools was family chronology, a therapeutic task that requires members of the client family to construct a time chart of significant events in the life span of the family. The family is instructed to include focal events, such as births, deaths, marriages, and divorces, as well as events that may have impacted the family in positive or negative ways, such as graduation, relocation, job loss, acquisition of a new job, and moving to a new city. Family chronology allows family members to view significant or influential events in sequence and thereby to gain a greater understanding of the context in which problems or issues may have emerged. The activity is done as an in-session task or as a homework assignment. In group work, members could develop their own life-span time charts, which might include family and other significant relationships in their lives as well as events affecting them and their families or significant others. The events included should reflect a balance of both positive and negative. Following completion of the charts, the group leader could encourage conversations about these events and their meanings, eliciting comments about the downside of "positive" events and the upside of the "negative" events (see Becvar & Becvar, 1994, p. 53).

Just as Satir used sculpting, enactments, and other experiences to help her clients understand the various communication stances (placating, blaming, super-reasonable, irrelevant, and congruent), similar work could be done in the context of a group. A variety of activities could be used to help group members become more open to experience. A ball of string could be used to help group members see how they are connected to each other and how they are connected and participate in the lives of people in their natural networks. In addition, members could be instructed to use sculpting to portray and choreograph certain vignettes from their relationships outside the group. A group member could be asked to sculpt a relationship vignette in the way that a specific person in his or her natural network might sculpt. In a couple's group, spouses could reciprocally sculpt and choreograph different vignettes from their lives together.

Any number of games, including popular board games, could be used to provide group members with tasks through which various relationship roles might be viewed and influenced. When playing these games, family or group members might be divided into teams in order to establish or diminish coalitions within the family or group. A benefit of the use of games is that the players accomplish a tangible task, and in the process they underscore family or group members' strengths and abilities. Variations of the use of games are limited only by the imagination and by the practical considerations of time and the composition of the family or group.

The way in which Satir used metaphor may also be relevant for group work. As employed by Satir, metaphor refers to a wide range of statements, stories, or tasks that lend themselves to symbolic representation on the part of the group members. Although all language is symbolic representation and therefore metaphoric, her use of "metaphor" referred to the intentional utilization of an event, verbal or nonverbal, that allowed clients to experience different meanings or interpretations. The power of the metaphor lay in the notion that there is no inherent meaning in any particular statement, story, or task. Similarly, in group work, group leaders could present a metaphor or task with no explanation, allowing group members to create their own meanings. In a sense, sculpting, family chronology, and games also provide experiences that allow different meanings and interpretations to emerge. In an even broader sense, any specific activity in the context of family therapy or group work is metaphoric.

Examples of some group activities that would be congruent with Satir's model follow.

- A group member could give another group member feedback on his or her communication stance(s) by sculpting the communication stance(s) that he or she experiences in the behavior of the other. The two group members could then discuss the experience. The leader would participate actively to ensure that the conversation is constructive in the spirit of Satir's approach.
- Group members could enact scenarios depicting relationships of individual group members with others outside the group (family choreography). The enactments would involve verbal and nonverbal behavior and movement. For example, two group members might enact a scene of how one of them greets her spouse when she comes home from work. There is an aspect of psychodrama in this activity although the processing would be directed to constructive discussions about the experience and empathy with the parties who participate in the experience. A complement to this activity would be to ask the focal group member to describe and choreograph how her husband probably experiences her upon his return home from work.
- Group members could play charades as a metaphor for expanding the range of experiences with which they might learn to be comfortable.
- Trust walks and trust falls might serve to open people to expanding their range of experience.
- A ball of string could be used to illustrate connectedness within a system. In this activity, one person would hold the end of the string and then toss the ball to another group member to whom he or she would direct a communication. The second group member, while holding onto the string and pulling it somewhat

taut, would then toss the ball to a third person, and so on, until a very complex web between people is created. Group members could poke at another person, hug another person, or in other ways interact with others, while holding onto the string to illustrate the way the whole is affected by their actions. The implicit message is that a person cannot do just one thing.

As you read our description of Satir's model, you may have felt the strong similarity between it and other humanistic approaches to counseling and group work. Although Satir's model is similar to some other approaches, it is also unique. Satir was one with her model, and it is highly unlikely that anyone else could do what she did in exactly the way she did it. Nor should they try. All of Satir's clients knew she was in charge, and they allowed her this influence for they experienced the deep caring, respect, and faith she showed them. Virginia Satir was a master therapist and teacher who taught didactically and experientially. Her model was an extension of herself. Nevertheless, there is much that therapists can learn from it and much that they can apply in their own work with individuals, couples, families, and groups.

# Murray Bowen's Family Systems Theory

Murray Bowen (1966, 1972, 1974, 1975, 1976, 1978) created a rich and coherent family therapy model, perhaps the only true theory among the many approaches to family systems therapy. It is clearly a first-order cybernetics approach in that the therapist is described as standing outside of the system, observing and diagnosing without intruding. Also in line with first-order cybernetics, it includes normative judgments about the degree of function and dysfunction in individuals, couples, and families. We believe that Bowen's model could be applied to developmental, preventive, and remedial group work.

Bowen's approach would be particularly useful in work that involves intensive one-to-one therapy in the context of a group. Indeed, Bowen used this approach in working with groups of couples. In addition, the approach would lend itself to work with groups of adult individuals with a common metaphor for their symptoms and with groups of individuals with a variety of metaphors for their symptoms.

Like all theories, Bowen's provides concepts and constructs that exist in relationship to one another and have a coherence with one another; that is, each is meaningful, and each is meaningful only in relationship to the others. The following is a brief summary of the key concepts and constructs of Bowen's theory.

Bowen used the concept of the nuclear family emotional system to describe the relationships between all people living in a household and the extended family, whether alive or dead, regardless of where they live. The family as an emotional system, Bowen felt, is universal and multigenerational. Although the therapist may work with either individuals or the nuclear family system, the emotional heritage of previous generations is alive and plays an important and continuing part in their lives.

Another concept in Bowen's theory, differentiation of self, comprises two kinds of differentiation: (a) differentiation of self from others, and (b) differentiation of feeling processes from intellectual processes. A logical complement to differentiation of self is the concept of fusion. Bowen believed that the relationship between these two concepts translates into a scale from functional to dysfunctional. Differentiation of self from emotional entanglements in the family of origin and the ability to differentiate within oneself between feeling and reasoning are both indicators of health. People who are able to differentiate in these ways, Bowen felt, can deal effectively with emotional entanglements and also are more flexible, adaptable, and self-sufficient. They feel their own feelings, and although they are sensitive to the feelings of others, they are objective and maintain a useful emotional distance. Having a rational, conscious awareness of the level of emotional entanglement in relationships, they can transcend such entanglements and thereby avoid them. Conversely, people who are unable to differentiate in these ways, or are fused, tend to be more rigid and more emotionally dependent upon others for their sense of well-being. They also have a difficult time maintaining objectivity.

Bowen also distinguished between solid-self and pseudo-self, a distinction that values the intellectual over the emotional. The solid-self person lives his or her life on a foundation of definite and carefully reasoned beliefs, opinions, convictions, and principles. The concept of pseudo-self relates to the concept of fusion. The pseudo-self person, or pretend self (which may be experienced as real), makes decisions relative to emotional pressure; he or she may make choices and decisions that are inconsistent without being aware of the inconsistency. The pseudo-self person's identity and sense of well-being are dependent upon others.

Another concept, multigenerational transmission process, is tied closely to differentiation of self and fusion. Bowen believed that people bring into a relationship varying degrees of differentiation and fusion from their families of origin, just as their parents brought into their relationship varying degrees of differentiation and fusion from their families of origin. Two undifferentiated people tend to find each other, and the family they create will become even more undifferentiated than were their own families of origin. Any attempts at emotional cutoff from their families of origin will increase the fusion between the spouses. The adults in this new family system tend to produce an unstable field in which each looks to the other for stability, for ways to respond emotionally, and for decisions regarding the making of choices. For the fused marital partners, this instability can lead to (a) reciprocal emotional distancing from each other; (b) the development of physical or emotional symptoms in one or both spouses; (c) marital conflict; and (d) the projection of problems, described as the family projection process, onto one or more of the children.

The family projection process logically fits the concept of the triangle or the process of triangulation. The dyadic relationship between spouses is stable as long as their situation is not stressful or the stress is transitory rather than chronic. According to Bowen, the degree of stress needed to destabilize the spousal system is relative to the degree of fusion, or lack of differentiation, of the spouses. However, chronic stress can upend the stability of all but the most differentiated spouses, although it can challenge even them. When the level of chronic or situational anxiety reaches a critical level, a vulnerable third party may be brought in, or triangulated. Thus, one spouse may turn to a child for support, forming a coalition with this child in conflicts with the other spouse. If the other spouse feels this coalition, he or she may turn to another child for support and as a counterbalance to the first spouse-child coalition. If the stress or anxiety is too great for these triangles, other triangles may be formed.

The paradox of this scenario is that although triangulation often occurs as an attempt to stabilize an unstable field, it actually serves to increase the instability. If a child is triangulated, the parent-child roles may become reversed in that the person who needs stability and assurance from parents is expected to provide it to a parent. If a child is triangulated by one parent, the child may become emotionally cut off from the other parent. As with the projection process, triangulation requires that the spouses collaborate. It takes two. No one spouse, or parent, is to blame.

If children become triangulated, they may cut themselves off emotionally, a survival method that may be logical but is ineffective. The concept of emotional cutoff describes attempts on the part of the children to differentiate, which may involve moving away from home when they become old enough, eliminating, reducing, or trying to control the kind of involvement they have with their families of origin, or both. According to Bowen, these attempts will fail because the children carry with them unresolved emotional attachments. Denial, isolation of self, and the development of a pseudo-self are all forms of emotional cutoff. Indeed, the more concerted the effort at emotional cutoff from the family of origin, the more there is indication of undifferentiation or fusion. As this scenario plays out over generations of the family, each new generation tends to become less differentiated and more fused with the emotional system that is the family. As mentioned earlier, Bowen called this process multigenerational transmission.

Bowen also wrote about the process of society. With this concept, Bowen extended his description of the emotional dynamics of the family to the emotional dynamics of the larger context. He described societies as being able to handle situational emotional stress more or less well. Chronic stress, however, poses a greater problem.

> Under conditions of chronic stress, both the family and the society will lose contact with their intellectually determined principles and will resort to an emotional basis for decisions that may offer short-term relief, but by these very attempts at short-term relief, may create more severe problems in the society as a result of these efforts. (Becvar & Becvar, 1996, pp. 152–153)

Bowen did not talk about abnormality and normality as being either present or absent in a person or family. Rather, he presented the concept of optimal functioning, where an individual's degree of functioning is based on his or her degree of differentiation and intellectual functioning. Bowen felt that complete and total differentiation and intellectual functioning do not exist in any person. Whether a person develops symptoms of dysfunction depends on two factors: the degree of differentiation from the family of origin and the level and chronicity of stress experienced.

In the ideal marriage, both spouses will have a high degree of differentiation of self and differentiation of emotion and intellectual functioning. In their role as parents, these spouses will be their own persons and will allow their children to be their own people, feel their own feelings, and be connected to both parents. Even in these families, with their high levels of differentiation, intense situational or chronic stress will be a challenge. However, these families will rebound quickly and will learn from the challenge to handle a wide range of problems. Triangulation is never absent, even in the best of families. Offhand remarks like, "Your dad is late again" or "We had better get home or your mom will be mad," made by a parent in the presence of a child, are forms of triangulation.

In summary, optimal individuals according to Bowen's theory are

> inner directed, establish their own goals, and assume responsibility for their own lives. These people relate to others out of strength rather than out of need. Although it is doubtful that anyone ever becomes fully differentiated, such individuals are rational, objective, and their own persons. They separate thinking from feeling and are able to remain independent of, though not necessarily out of contact with, the nuclear and extended family. To Bowen, self-differentiation was a lifelong search for intrapersonal freedom and thus for satisfying interpersonal relationships. (Becvar & Becvar, 1996, p. 154)

# Applying Bowen's Model to Group Work

As mentioned earlier, Bowen did not work with whole families. He worked with individual adults and with couples. Part of his rationale for working with individual adults and couples rather than families likely reflected his systemic belief that change comes from the inside out, or through individuals who can affect other family members. He believed that the process of individuation, which begins as a personal, individual process, ultimately affects all other members of the family system. Thus, group leaders, even though working one-to-one with individuals, would need to think in terms of whole systems to be consistent with this model.

Group leaders adhering to this model would focus on processes rather than on specific issues. Their therapeutic stance would be rational and intellectual, reflecting a naturalistic research design in which observations are made from a neutral position. By being rational and intellectual, they also would avoid being triangulated. Metaphors describing group leaders' roles would include coach, consultant, and teacher. They would move people toward intellectual processing and away from emotionality, which, according to this approach, is the problem. They also might teach clients about systems and the multigenerational transmission process.

A tool they might employ is the genogram, using it to help clients take an observer stance relative to their families of origin. The questions asked would require intellectual or rational rather than emotional answers. Throughout this type of activity, group leaders would maintain emotional distance, with knowledge of the family projection process and triangulation helping them to maintain this distance. By maintaining their emotional distance, group leaders would help members also gradually develop emotional distance from their families of origin as they learn about family projection processes and triangulation.

Although the group leader would be doing one-to-one work with individual members of the group, other group members would learn vicariously by observing the leader's work with individual members. Although there might be similarities between families, there are always differences, and those differences would have to be respected.

Whether working with groups of individuals with common metaphors for their problems or with couples, the group leader would initially focus on allowing intense emotions to be expressed. His or her responses to the expressed emotions would help to move the members to articulate the thoughts underlying their feelings rather than responding to the feelings. Recall that it is the intense expressed emotion that indicates undifferentiation and fusion. With couples, expressed emotions tend to recycle previous unsuccessful attempts at problem solving and lead to projection of responsibility to the other spouse. Emotionality is expected in this type of therapy but is not viewed as useful therapeutically. When couples begin to experience their relationship from an intellectual, rational perspective, they may be able to solve problems effectively for the first time. They may begin to listen well. All questions asked by the leader would reflect a calm, neutral, rational posture designed to elicit information about thoughts about self and others. Emotionality is the problem; it is not the solution.

When the group members' emotionality has been reduced, and individual members or groups of couples have begun to move toward an intellectual, objective stance relative to their families of origin and each other, the group leader would begin to teach them about their level of differentiation either directly or indirectly, using the language and concepts from the theory. At this point a genogram (see Becvar & Becvar, 1996, pp. 156–157; Guerin & Pendagast, 1976, p. 452; McGoldrick & Gerson, 1985) also might be used.

The genogram is a tool that provides individuals with a visual map of their extended families. In the group context, genograms would begin with the focal group member or the focal couple and would then extend backward for as many generations as possible. The group leader would pose questions that would seek intellectual responses to help the individuals see patterns and relationships. The genograms could include information about cultural and ethnic origins, socio-economic status, religion, physical location (which includes information about the proximity of family members), as well as the frequency and kind of contact between the individual and family members and information about contact between other family members. Dates of death, marriage, and other significant events would also be included on the genograms. The group leader might ask questions about the group members' perspectives on the relative health of different relationships as well as their degree of openness, degree of emotionality, and rules regarding emotionality and triangulation. Developing genograms could be a group activity. However, if the activity is done this way, the group leader's generic questions might miss important aspects of the unique emotional system that is each family. Thus, the activity would probably best be completed one-on-one in the context of the group. If genograms are done as a simultaneous group activity, the group leader should follow up with specific questions to each group member.

After attaining more of an observer stance relative to their families of origin and their own level of differentiation of self, the group members would need to take the next step in the process of differentiating—going home again or going home again differently as their attempts at emotional cutoff do not work. However, going home again does not mean getting into confrontation, nor does it mean reconciliation or establishing peace and harmony. It means taking the intellectual, rational, observer stance and gathering information about family systems with and from the members of those systems. It means getting to know other family members by listening, which is best done one-on-one. A basic systemic notion is that one-on-one conversations are different kinds of conversations than those that occur with three people present. Issues can be addressed in one-on-one conversations, but the participants must maintain their own intellectual, rational stance and not get hooked. Group members would be challenged to trust the process and model what they have learned in the group.

Going home also may involve increasing the frequency of phone calls, visits, or letters to family members. The leader might coach group members on how to write letters and how to conduct themselves in conversations in a way that would maintain and increase their level of differentiation. A part of this coaching might involve helping group members extricate themselves from triangles in their families of origin. Family members would notice the difference in group members' behavior and probably would resist the change and attempt to hook the members back into their previous roles. Group leaders could help members maintain their new stance and increase their movement toward differentiation. The process of detriangulation may involve taking positions similar to the following:

- Having conversations and building different kinds of relationships with the other two parties in the triangle. The new relationships may alienate the one with whom the individual group member was in coalition, but this alienation is usually very temporary.
- Refusing to talk about third parties in conversations with either of the other two parties in the triangle. Statements like, "That's between you and Dad" and "That's an issue you need to discuss with Jane," could be used.
- Listening to Mom's comments about Dad and reporting to Dad what Mom is saying about him, and vice versa. This stance, while it may feel risky, will certainly challenge the existing family pattern. Indeed, the two parents may confront each other and end up forming a coalition against the child.

If the group members were couples, they could learn to maintain their intellectual, rational stance with each other and thus help each other differentiate. This intellectual, rational stance might help them attain a higher degree of constructive emotional closeness and intimacy than either had experienced before or even thought possible. But each member of the couple would have to go home again in a way similar to that described for individuals. However, this going home would be different from that for individuals in that each would feel the other's support. Couples could thus learn to coach each other.

As mentioned earlier, the move toward differentiation of self is a lifelong process. Accordingly, a group of individuals or couples that met with this goal might not end; it might merely stretch out the times between meetings. The group could continue to be a support system for the never-ending journey.

# In Conclusion

At this point, we end our overview of first-order cybernetic family therapy models and their application to group work. Although there are several other models that we also could have reviewed, our intent was to demonstrate how first-order cybernetic models might be used in group work. We challenge you to look more broadly at the models we selected, as well as others, in this regard. Now, however, it is time to continue the conversation by moving into the world of second-order cybernetics and social constructionism. To that end, we will see what kind of fit we can create between these perspectives and group therapy and examine specific techniques that might be useful and applicable to group work.

# 6

## Second-Order Cybernetics/ Constructivism, Social Constructionism, and Group Work

*I*n this chapter we explore therapeutic approaches that we believe are consistent with the postmodern philosophical tradition. Second-order cybernetics/constructivism and social constructionism both fit (more or less well) under this umbrella. In our view, second-order cybernetics/constructivism and social constructionism complement each other in their shared focus on the therapy process as reflexive and collaborative. From all of these frameworks, knowing and knowledge are social constructions; language and social discourse, as well as the process of intersubjective, shared meaning-making, are key areas of concern. In addition, these perspectives are nonnormative and in fundamental ways challenge normative psychology and mental health practice in the modernist tradition. Indeed, an important aspect of social constructionism is the study of the "construction of stories and narratives, from both a micro and macro level" (Gale & Long, 1995).

Among the approaches we review in this chapter are those of Tom Andersen, Harry Goolishian and Harlene Anderson, and Michael White and David Epston, all of which often are classified in the family therapy literature as second-order therapies (Hoffman, 1985). Whereas first-order therapies (those in accord with first-order cybernetics) involve deliberate, conscious intention from the stance of an expert consistent with a social engineering position, second-order therapies involve therapists who seek consciously to be reflexive, nonnormative, collaborative, and nonhierarchical. Second-order therapists also consciously strive to be nonpathologizing, nonobjectifying, noncontrolling, curious, and respectful.

Some second-order cyberneticians/constructivists and social constructionists (e.g., Atkinson & Heath, 1990a, 1990b; Atkinson, 1992) believe that normative thinking and assessment are inevitable and that first-order modes of intervention can be utilized without objectifying and pathologizing. For example, Atkinson (1992, p. 389) stated, "Therapists cannot avoid normative thinking and instrumentalism at some level.... The issue is how therapists communicate their normative values and influence clients, not whether they do." Further, Atkinson and Heath (1990b, p. 145) noted, "Second-order cybernetics in no way replaces the validity of first-order cybernetics. Rather they are related in complementary fashion. Ideally, pragmatic strategies gleaned from first-order thinking are contextualized by the aesthetic concerns of second-order cybernetics." Whereas a first-order cybernetician attempts to understand what is "really" going on or what the "real" problem is, the second-order cybernetician views himself or herself as a participant in creating a universe of experience (Keeney, 1982).

In this chapter we also review the solution-focused model of Steve de Shazer and Insoo Berg, whose approach to therapy has a first-order cybernetics feel and yet seems philosophically consistent with social constructionism. Their approach deconstructs the problem-solving methods found in most traditional mental health practice and constructs solution-oriented problem-solving methods.

Before we begin our review of selected models, we present a generic script of self-talk by a group leader whose orientation is second-order cybernetics/constructivism and social constructionism. In this conversation with herself, the group leader is aware of the various aspects of first-order cybernetics, second-order cybernetics/constructivism, and social constructionism. Through this script we hope to illustrate the basic concepts of second-order cybernetics/constructivism and social constructionism in the thinking of a group leader.

# Self-Talk About Group Work

Although group members bring some roles, attitudes, and behaviors with them to the group, how they are in the group reflects how I am with them and how the members of the group are with each other and with me.

As I listen to group members' stories about themselves and their problems, it is important that I be consciously aware of the story I am telling myself about them and their problem-saturated stories. Moreover, I must also be aware that there are many possible stories I could tell myself about them and their stories and that I cannot know which of these stories is the "true" story about them and the problems they describe as experiencing.

I use the "screening" interview to gain information for selecting members for the group, but I am aware that the people I am interviewing are also "selecting." Through the conversation and mutual interactions that occur, the screening and selecting process marks the beginning of the cocreation of a therapeutic reality.

As I listen to potential group members during the screening/selecting process, I am likely to hear one or more of the standardized, problem-saturated stories that have evolved from the professional literature. Members may come in search of a symptom-focused treatment for their "problem" metaphor, which fits their problem-saturated story—a story that may be living their lives for them. Because of my second-order cybernetics/constructivist and social constructionist perspective, I may challenge this idea in fundamental ways.

I am aware that the prospective clients will become aware directly or indirectly about my second-order cybernetics/constructivist and social constructionist way of thinking and doing therapy as I converse with them. In this process of mutual perturbation I will get some idea of how each prospective participant is structurally determined.

As I think about the possibility of constituting the group around a common metaphor for their "problem" (delinquency, substance abuse, divorce), I am aware that if I use a standardized symptom-focused approach, my apparent belief in it and my facilitating the group based on this approach will participate in the reification of the metaphor and give group members little choice except to search for a solution within the confines of the standardized symptom-focused treatment.

As a second-order cybernetician/constructivist and social constructionist, my challenge is to work with the group members to deconstruct their problem-saturated stories and related stories about how problems get solved and to cocreate new stories, rather than to diagnose from one frame of reference. My hope is that together we will find a fit that structurally couples with the nervous system of each member around change in such a way that the problem is solved or dis-solved. Each group member's internal structure, or nervous system, defines the behaviors of which that individual is capable and defines which alternative stories will fit. Each member of the group will have a different internal structure, so I cannot make a decision about which story will structurally couple with each group member in advance or independent of the group member. A story must evolve in dialogue with each group member.

Because I cannot know in advance nor can I decide independent of each group member which theory, story, activity, or metaphor may fit that person, I must listen to each person's story and as much as possible refrain from telling myself my own story about the client and his or her problem-saturated story. I must listen with an attitude of neutrality, feeling "a sense of compassion, interest, and curiosity" about each group member's dilemma. As others have put it, I must ask myself, "How did they get where they are? How did they organize themselves that way?" and I must "try to see the logic even in situations that I find repugnant from a moral point of view" (Boscolo, Cecchin, Hoffman, & Penn, 1987, p. 152).

I must also be aware of my observing system stance and acknowledge the inevitability that I will edit while listening and observing. Through the questions I will ask and my choice of material for mirroring, for paraphrase, or for empathy, I cannot help but influence the nature of the story that each group member presents. The stories people tell about themselves are audience- or context-specific.

As I listen and respond to each group member, I must carefully observe him or her to gain feedback about the goodness of fit of my editing with his or her structure. If I succumb to the temptation to listen to my story about what I believe is "really" going on, I will not receive this feedback from the group member. The dialogues between myself and each group member and between group members should be experienced by all as mutual perturbation.

If I am alert to this feedback from group members about my editing and other perturbations, I may push, confront, or otherwise try to persuade group members into the truth of my story and in the process will create the interpersonal process that has been called resistance. I must remember that I will perceive resistance only if I believe in that concept and if I push or pull too hard. My observation of "resistance" only suggests that my perturbation did not structurally fit the group member. Observing "resistance" says as much, if not more, about me than it does about the group member.

To be consistent with second-order cybernetics in my group work, I must facilitate (or impose) process goals, which each group member must learn if the group is to have coherence. Although I am aware that the establishment of norms in the context of a group is inevitable, for it is consistent with the concept "group," I also recognize that such group norms are an inconsistency from the perspective of second-order cybernetics, which suggests that theories and change processes must be respectful of the uniqueness of each group member. I can alleviate this dilemma to some extent by being transparent about the values and assumptions implicit in my framework.

If I decide to use the group context for remediation or problem resolution, I must be respectful of and consistent with my second-order cybernetics perspective whenever the process I am facilitating does not structurally fit any or all group members. Likewise, I must respect the decision by any or all group members not to continue in the group without finding fault with that group member.

Although being transparent and open feels right and fair to me, I am also aware of the paradox of seductive power that accompanies the process of "facilitating" and being "transparent" and "open."

I cannot know what would be helpful to individual members of the group. Although they may come to the group with a common metaphor about their dilemma or problem, each is unique. I must respect this uniqueness. My aesthetic and my ethic are that any story we cocreate must fit and respect the unique life situation of each group member.

I must be sensitive to the possibility that some group members may not feel they have a dilemma or problem, and I know I must not get hooked into persuading them that they do have a dilemma or problem. My challenge is to get some idea about why they chose to participate in the group and, if the group is not a good fit, to help them find an experience that may be useful for them.

The process I envision is one of working with clients to cocreate stories that are different from the ones in which they are currently living their lives (or the ones that are living their lives for them). I can draw on many resources, including classical theories of therapy and personality, theories of family therapy, and stories from world literature, the humanities, the theater, and so forth. But the test for the utility of any story is its appropriateness for the client. No story that I select should pathologize or create normative standards.

*   *   *

We hope that this script will provide general context for the discussion that follows, in which we share some rationales and suggestions, consistent with second-order cybernetics/constructivism and social constructionism, for interventions and perturbations at different stages in the life of a group. At the same time, we recognize that it is inconsistent to speak of stages from these perspectives, according to which the group would just evolve. We realize that punctuating stages necessarily creates expectations about the pace of the group and the kinds of activities that "should" occur in specific stages, which cannot not create that reality.

# Rationales and Perturbations During the Beginning Stage

We feel it is important to reiterate that the group leader's thinking about the group process, described in the script just presented, would not change relative to the problem metaphors that members bring to a group. According to the second-order cybernetic and social constructionist perspective, although homogeneous grouping by symptom-focused metaphor is the norm in most group work, there is no theoretical reason why symptom-focused metaphors cannot be mixed in a group.

With that said, we move on to a discussion of second-order cybernetics and the leader's role at the beginning stage of a group. We begin with the screening process, during which many structural, procedural, and compositional questions are addressed. As important as these questions are, from a postmodernist perspective other issues that are equally if not more important also must be considered during the process of screening. As described in Chapter 3, these issues include the following:

- Discerning (creating) a "need" or "problem" that may define the purpose of the group
- Deciding that the group context is a better context for serving that purpose than are other experiences
- Selecting members for the group and informing members of the advantages and risks they may experience by their participation
- Selecting a theoretical model and related process goals to guide therapeutic discourse in the group
- Being aware of the possibility of creating more serious problems by attempting to meet the need or solve the problem that defines the purpose of the group (here, the group leader must think about the goodness of fit for people who are ethnically, racially, or culturally different, as well as for women, gays, and lesbians)
- Being aware of how change in group members may affect other people in the group members' natural contexts
- Being aware of the possible reification in the group of the metaphor describing the "need" or problem

The screening interview is also an opportunity for prospective group members to ask questions and to determine whether they will select this group experience. The emotional tone of the screening/selecting interview should be conversational rather than diagnostic. The leader should be transparent about the balance between risks and benefits, his or her theoretical orientation, and the process goals. By asking some or all of the following questions, the leader may help the prospective group members make an informed decision about joining the group. In addition, through these questions the group leader will introduce the idea of life as a storied reality.

- What is your story about your experienced need for professional assistance?
- What is your story about the problem, need, or dilemma you feel you need to address?
- Who in your life has told you that you have a problem in need of solution?
- What is your story about seeking counseling at this time?
- What is your story about coming to see me about group therapy?
- What is your story about selecting group therapy rather than an alternative?

- If you end up having a successful group experience, how would you be different?
- What is your story about what the group experience will be like?
- Who in your life would be most pleased if you were to accomplish your purpose in coming to group therapy?
- Who would be most disappointed if you were to change?
- What are your expectations for this group experience?
- What would you like to know that would help you decide about whether this group experience would be appropriate for you?
- From the description I have given you of what the group experience may be like and what will be expected of you, what fits for you and what does not fit for you?

Through these questions, prospective group members will learn to talk of stories and opinions rather than facts, a necessary process goal if one is to be consistent with the postmodern view of constructed realities. In asking these questions—indeed, throughout the screening interview—the leader does not come across as an expert. The screening interview thus provides an experience of what it would be like to be a group member.

The leader might well start the group with some typical getting-acquainted activities. Any number of activities could be used here, but one like the following would help members not only get acquainted but also learn to think about themselves as living their lives in stories.

> Welcome! I've met each of you and each of you has met me, but you haven't met each other. So let's take a few minutes and tell each other some stories that may help us to get acquainted.

The leader expects that the stories each member tells about him- or herself in the context of the group will be somewhat different from the stories he or she told in the screening interview, for storytelling is context- and audience-relative. In addition, the leader may solicit other stories:

- What is your story about your "need" for assistance?
- What is your story about the problem, need, or dilemma you feel you have?
- Who in your life tells you that you have a problem in need of solution?

- What stories do others tell themselves and you about your problem?

He or she also may solicit stories about members' goals for the group experience:

- If you were to be successful in this group, how would you be different?
- If you were to be successful in this group, what would you be doing more of, less of, or differently when you leave the group?
- If you were to be successful in this group, what would others notice about you that would be different?

A part of the orientation provided by the leader in the first meeting might be a formal introductory statement like that described by Atkinson (1992):

> Before we begin our sessions together, I want to be clear about how I view the counseling process. First, in the field of psychotherapy, I don't think we ever talk about facts. We talk about opinions. I think it's likely that if you went to five different therapists this week with the same problem, you might very well get five different ideas about why the problem exists or what can be done about it. If a therapist tells you, "It's obvious that this is the problem..." I believe that you should be skeptical. You should also know that there are therapists who disagree with me about this and who really do believe their judgments are objective. I'm just telling you that I don't believe that their ideas or mine are objective. This doesn't mean that I don't think that the ideas of therapists are valuable. Any one of these five therapists might be very helpful to you, but they may each proceed under five different assumptions. I have accumulated a certain amount of experience in this profession, I've read widely, and I've developed a certain group of assumptions and opinions about how to make sense of problems and what to do about them. I'll tell you honestly what I'm doing and thinking as we go along. Sometimes I get pretty enthusiastic about my ideas, and you'll probably sense this. I suggest that you always try to keep in mind that no matter how animated I get, these are just my ideas, not facts, and I'd like you to judge them on their own merits. Please feel free to disagree with me and tell me what you think. The most useful ideas in this process may occur to you, not me. (pp. 390–391)

To such an introduction we might add the following to bring the focus on to group work:

Everyone in this group shares a common problem or dilemma, or at least each of you has given or were assigned a common name to a problem you experience or that others have suggested that you have. This is what brings us together. The fact that you share a common problem or dilemma does not mean that you are all alike, nor does it mean that there is a common solution to the problem or dilemma you share. Indeed, as we get to know one another, you may find that although all of you may give your problem or dilemma a common name, there may be important differences between you. A solution for one of you may or may not be a solution for others in the group. I know that each of you is unique, and I shall endeavor to respect your uniqueness in my work with you.

In our group sessions, I will work intensively with each of you one-on-one. Other members of the group may participate in my work with each of you; however, I ask that anyone who does participate join me in my style of working. This group must be a safe place. We can make it a safe place by respecting the guidelines I have just described. We can also make it safe by respecting that what is said in here should stay in here. This is called confidentiality. We can make it safer still by not talking with another member outside the group about a third member of the group.

Such general introductory statements are intended to formally orient group members to the metatheory of second-order cybernetics/constructivism and social constructionism. A discussion among the group members could follow. Of course, not all group leaders would choose such a formal orientation. Indeed, the formal orientation is countercultural in that it challenges the modernist expectations of group members that the group leader be the expert and that there is a universal model for treatment that applies to all group members.

The group leader might continue his or her introductory remarks by discussing another important aspect of both first- and second-order cybernetics that will come into play in the group:

I don't do "whys." I believe it is important that the focus of our work together be on what can be done about the problem, not on why the problem exists or persists. I don't believe we can know the real "why."

The leader might then get the members involved in the discussion by reactivating the belief in life as a storied reality. The leader's intervention could take the following form:

> As you listened to everyone tell stories about themselves, their problems, and other people in their lives as well as the stories these other people tell themselves about them, what stories were activated in you about the other person and yourself?

The leader might begin the processing of the first storytelling experience to provide a model for the others to follow. His or her statements could be some variation on the following:

> The story I am telling myself about Sam after hearing his story(ies) is_____.

> As I listened to Sam's story(ies), the story I was telling myself about myself was _____.

The culmination of the beginning stage might include a discussion with group members about the goodness of fit of their experience in the first group session with their objectives for the group. The group leader might introduce the discussion as follows:

> Before we end this first meeting, I would like to ask you to share your story of your experience in the group today. I am particularly interested in hearing about the fit of your experience with your expectations for the group and the possibilities for meeting your objectives in the group. I am especially interested in hearing whether you will continue with the group. If you choose not to continue, I will respect your decision and work with you to find an experience that you feel might be a better fit for you.

Whatever responses group members might give to this request, the leader must ensure that a spirit consistent with a postmodernist perspective prevails. That is, the client is the expert in his or her life and is respected. His or her story is the first story. The leader must always be aware of the group context and the pressure for conformity that a group can create.

Finally, the leader may want to contract for a specific number of sessions with those members who choose to continue in the group.

However, it is important to keep in mind that from the second-order cybernetics/constructivist and social constructionist perspectives, therapy takes as long as it takes. Proponents of these perspectives would not view the therapy process in the long-term/brief therapy dichotomy that is so prevalent in the professional literature. When each group member has received what he or she came for, the therapy is finished for that person. Along the same line, each group member is the expert who decides whether he or she has received what he or she came for.

Second-order cybernetics/constructivist and social constructionist approaches could pose problems for group members who have been socialized into the view of the therapist as an expert who diagnoses, categorizes, and distributes along a scale and thereby compares and contrasts people. They may expect certainty from the therapist, as well as a specific symptom-focused treatment for *the* problem after *the* diagnosis. This view, promoted by mental health practice in the modernist tradition, has become a part of the commonsense psychology and therapy of the consumer. By contrast, the postmodernist group leader is an expert in building relationships, in language, in respecting uniqueness, and in deconstructing old and creating new stories. Group members would need to be socialized into this alternate view either directly or indirectly.

The rationales and suggestions described in this section are not exhaustive, nor are the suggestions we provide for the work stage in the life of the group. They are simply illustrative of modes of thinking and interventions consistent with our interpretation of second-order cybernetics/constructivism and social constructionism.

# Rationales and Perturbations During the Work Stage

So what, from this framework, does the therapist do in the process or work stage in the life of a group? The answer is specific and yet general. The therapist can do almost anything consistent with the basic precepts of second-order cybernetics/constructivism and social constructionism. He or she can also draw upon ideas from first-order cybernetics; however, the therapist must bear in mind that unlike a first-order cybernetician who believes it is possible to understand what "really" is going on or what the "real" problem is, the postmodernist views himself or herself as a participant in creating a universe of experience (Keeney, 1982) and speaks of opinions rather than facts. A key question the therapist would need to consider is, what is the difference that will make a difference with each unique group member with his or her unique problem?

Some other important questions the therapist would need to consider include the following: How does one change a story? How does one change the stories group members may tell themselves about others in their lives? How does one change the stories that others in each group member's network tell themselves about the group member? What is the history of the stories told?

Our response to these questions is that stories are always changing, for they are audience- or context-relative. The story that each person tells about himself or herself changes as he or she tells it to a job interviewer, to a friend, to a colleague at work, to a spouse. Stories also change when the audience asks different questions. Recall Atkinson's observation about five different therapists each of whom would elicit and create a different story from the client relative to the theoretical orientation of the therapist. So, as therapists ask different questions, stories are retold in different ways. As will become evident when we describe specific approaches, most postmodern therapists utilize questions, thereby participating in the creation of different and hopefully more useful stories.

In addition, as therapists edit different pieces of an individual's story via paraphrase, empathy, or mirroring, stories are told differently. As they edit by nodding or not nodding to selected aspects of a group member's story, the story changes. As a function of all of these behaviors, the therapist moves further along in the process of becoming of one mind with the group member. As the group member and therapist watch each other and together choreograph a recursive dance, they move closer to becoming one system. But this process of cocreation is aborted when a group member experiences an attempted unilateral move from the therapist as expert. From this perspective, nonintervention is not possible; indeed, the interventions and perturbations can be empowering in that the client has the final word regarding their utility.

For example, the therapist can influence a change in story by providing the storyteller with different experiences. Perhaps the most profound means for transforming a story a group member may tell about him- or herself and others is through allowing the group member to experience respect and acceptance consistent with second-order cybernetics/constructivism and social constructionism. As the group leader helps group members become aware of their own expertise about their lives, their stories about self and others may change.

Therapists also can change a story by telling stories about themselves, about other clients, or about topics that may indirectly or directly have relevance to the client's situation. As Combs and Freedman (1990, p. 39) put it, "because metaphor is indirect, multidimensional, and multimeaningful, [storytelling] is a communication form that incorporates some randomness." The use of storytelling is thus a stochastic process. One does not know and cannot predict which story will be meaningful to which group member. A story told in a conversation with group member *A* may resonate with group member *B*. Even if the group leader tells a story with a specific purpose in mind, group members may give it their own meaningful twist. Storytelling is not a commonsense therapy activity in the modernist tradition (except for theory-specific interpretations); but post modernists would contend that storytelling, if done frequently during a group session, can be an expected, appreciated, and useful part of the group process.

As you read about the different approaches that can be used in the process stage of a group, you will become aware, as noted earlier, of an almost universal reliance on questions. Questions are used both to deconstruct stories and to create new stories. As Alan Watts (1972, p. 34) noted, "Problems that remain persistently insoluble should always be suspected as questions asked in the wrong way." As the group leader asks different questions, different stories and different solutions become possible.

Although the therapist and group members may have contracted for a specific number of meetings, each group meeting is treated as a first as well as potentially a last session. Continuity from the previous to the current session may occur but is not assumed. Any discussions the therapist may have with self or others between group meetings about the group, including considerations of what to do in the next meeting, would assume continuity. As such, they may lead to an agenda relative to where group members were and where the group leader thinks they may be, not where they are. Given the ideas and assumptions just described, a general opening like one of the following would better fit during the work stage:

Would each of you tell us about where you are today?

Tell us some stories about your life since our last meeting.

On the basis of the information obtained from each group member, previously planned activities might fit, but they should not be forced to fit. The leader is not interested in where the group is but in where each individual member of the group is. The latter would be the starting point of the leader's conversation with each person.

Because the leader is not promoting a specific symptom-focused treatment, much of the therapeutic work in the session is one-to-one. Other group members become an audience for each conversation. As an audience, they may find some parts of the conversation meaningful for them. However, the leader's focus is on the individual with whom he or she is having a conversation, rather than on what the audience is hearing. Other group members may participate in this conversation if their participation is consistent with the attitude of second-order cybernetics/constructivism and social constructionism. That is, the leader views any group member's contributions as potentially useful if those contributions do not pathologize or engage in searches for whys; they must offer encouragement and hope and not be delivered in the tone of an expert. Thus, each group member is expected to behave in a manner consistent with that of the leader.

After an opening such as those suggested here, a leader might ask:

Who would like to be the first person to have a conversation with me today?

Again, the group leader would not diagnose or assess the client in any formal way. To do so would be to disempower the client by assigning a deficit story to an experience. In addition, the process of formal diagnosis and assessment would place the therapist in a hierarchical position as the expert whose word is final and definitive. Rather, as Gergen and Kaye (1992) suggested, the appropriate professional posture is one of "not knowing" and of taking a "de-expertized" position. We do not mean to suggest that clinicians do not have some alternative stories that may be useful. However, the way a clinician may convey his or her "knowledge" is through his or her relationship with the client, whose "knowledge" and stories are considered to be equally valid to those of the clinician. Thus, the clinician seeks to empower the client through the establishment of a more egalitarian or collaborative relationship. Such a relationship is more likely to be experienced as a conversation than as a therapy session. This empowerment is especially important with clients who have internalized a totalizing, deficit story and whose lives are being lived by that story.

The therapist also is curious and respectful, much like an ethnographic researcher who searches for and seeks to understand the multiple stories (rather than the true story) that make up the local culture. He or she views each client system as a unique culture that deserves to be understood from within its own framework instead of according to the categories of the ethnographer's culture. Indeed, as Cecchin (1992, p. 91) noted, curiosity and respect "provide the opportunity for the construction of new forms of action and interpretation."

Another guideline for practitioners from a postmodernist perspective relates to the way information is shared. That is, the therapist offers his or her "knowledge" tentatively rather than definitively, as ideas on which the client may reflect for possible utility. Andersen (1991) suggested that the ideas offered by a therapist should be positive and should imply and activate client strengths. Hopes, preferences, values, and opinions can be offered, but they should be relayed on the basis of personal experience rather than on authority or expertise. For, from this perspective, professional ideas are no more valid or "true" than those of the client. Further, the therapy process is collaborative and is based on the fundamental assumptions that there are as many ideas as there are people giving voice to them and that each person may have several ideas about the "same" situation. Multiple ideas open multiple possibilities. Laird (1995) listed the following questions as openings the therapist could use to help plant the idea of living one's life in a story and to help create the reality that multiple ideas are possible:

> Does this set of meanings reflect your experiences as lived? Does the story constrain or open up possibilities for you? Does this story of your life foster self-disparagement? Self-blaming? Hopelessness? Does it diminish opportunities for you to achieve your full potential? Does it prevent you from taking responsibility for your actions? Does it preclude action altogether? Does it isolate you or others from possible resources? How did you learn this way of being a woman? A man? Are there other possible interpretations for what happened to you? (p. 157)

Many other questions also might be asked. The important thing to remember is that no story is ever fixed. The story one tells is relative to the audience and will fit the attitude and questions the audience brings to the conversation. Thus, the story one tells is reflexive. In White's (1991) terms, storytelling is an opportunity to "reauthor" one's life. The conversation in therapy "is the act of making oneself an object of one's own observation" (Lax, 1992, p. 75). And the focus is on discovering one's strengths and resources and on feeling empowered to author one's own life and to find the "exceptions" and "unique outcomes" that challenge all pervasive and debilitating deficit stories.

Although history may be elicited, that information is used for perspective and is not understood to be constant. It, too, is seen as evolving relative to the audience. Rather than being a series of events, the history behind a story is the story about the events, and that story is always relative to the interpreter and the persons for whom he or she is interpreting. Further, in the context of therapy, the history behind a story undoubtedly will be replete with many stories of negative events and will be designed to fit the client's story about what is expected in therapy.

Therapists working from a postmodernist perspective are not limited to questions. Nor, as noted previously, does therapy from this perspective preclude utilizing strategic ideas, techniques, and processes from a first-order cybernetics perspective. As Hoffman (1993, pp. 153–154) wrote, "I do not reject the more instrumental approaches in the family therapy field. Even though the stance I use may seem nondirective, there is nothing in it that says I should not give people concrete tasks and interpretations as long as I make it clear that I am only giving the 'idea of' a task or interpretation."

Having provided a general introduction to the postmodernist perspective as it relates to the beginning and work stages of a group, we now move to a consideration of some specific second-order family therapy approaches and their application to group work.

# Tom Andersen's Reflecting Team

Tom Andersen (1987, 1991, 1992, 1993) and his Norwegian associates developed an approach to family therapy based on the key question, "Why did we hide away [in family therapy sessions] our deliberations about the families?" (Andersen, 1992, p. 57). The answer, that there is no good or respectful reason to do so unless one assumes the position of an expert, reveals their philosophy, in which they make a distinction between "public language" and "private language." Private language, according to their approach, is that of professionals, intellectuals, and academicians. By contrast, they sought to move from "professional language toward daily language" (Andersen, 1992, p. 58), or language that could be articulated to clients and that promotes a common understanding. This move was seen as a means of empowering clients and introduced a participant-observer, rather than an expert, stance on the part of the therapist. Thus, the idea of a reflecting team was born.

In this approach, the family is fully informed that a reflecting team, made up of professionals, will observe the session and is invited to meet the members of the team. After a time (generally 15 to 45 minutes into the session), the therapist might say, "I wonder if the team at this point has any ideas that might be helpful. May I ask them if they have?" (Andersen, 1987, p. 420). The family members would then move to an observer position, as they listen to the professionals share their observations of the family members and their relationships as well as related ideas. Professional reflections in "private language" would not be helpful, and therefore all reflections are presented in public language.

A key question for Andersen regarding how people change was, how much difference is too much or too little? Too little difference will not be helpful. Too much difference may lead to the disintegration of the system. To find answers to this question, the therapist and observers must become sensitive to the clients' level of participation and demonstrated comfort and discomfort.

Another important observation made by Andersen was that when professionals observing a family session talked to one another using private or professional language, they tended to come up with fewer ideas than when they observed silently. Thus, the reflecting team observes silently, that is, without conversations with one another. It is also important that their reflections describe what they have observed in the family therapy session—"When I heard..." or "When I saw...I thought about..."—and that they offer their observations tentatively rather than definitively. For example, they may say, "I am not sure, however it seems that..." or "When I saw that I wondered...." Observations made in this manner allow clients to select a reflection that fits them from the menu offered. Equally possible and equally important is for clients to choose not to listen.

In addition, the reflections should have positive rather than negative connotations and should include speculation of possibilities, for, as Andersen stated, "Nothing is negative in itself; it becomes negative when the listener perceives it to be negative" (1992, p. 60). A team member might say, for example, "I wonder what the result would be if they tried..." In addition, when sharing their reflections, team members are to look at one another rather than at the family members, an action aimed at reducing the pressure family members may feel to accept what they hear. Thus, the reflections should have the quality of tentative offerings, give no normative judgments, carry a positive connotation, communicate both-and or neither-nor rather than either-or messages, and be connected to the verbal and nonverbal information the observers noted in the preceding conversation. Further, the team's reflecting style should seek to approximate the family members' own mode of reflecting (i.e., the rhythm, speed, and style of communication). The team also may speculate on what would happen if anything in the picture changed or if an alternative explanation were accepted. "The team must be positive, discreet, respectful, sensitive, imaginative, and creatively free" (Andersen, 1987, p. 424). These attributes would also describe the attitude and demeanor of the therapist who is working directly with the family.

After the reflecting team concludes its task, the family is given the opportunity to reflect on the reflections. The therapist would solicit the family members' reactions to what they saw and heard. The approach is based on the assumption that the family will select those ideas that fit and that those ideas may influence the creation of a small change in the family's picture or in its understanding. The therapist also may share any ideas stimulated by the reflections of the team.

The reflecting team may be used as a resource several times during a session. However, the last word is always between the therapist and family.

# Applying Andersen's Approach to Group Work

Although it was developed for work with families, the reflecting team model could be used in remedial work with groups of individuals, couples, or families. Staying consistent with the model, the therapist could conduct a one-to-one interview with each group member either in the context of the group or in front of a one-way mirror with the rest of the group observing. After a time the group member who was interviewed could be invited to hear the ideas of other group members. The protocol set forth by Andersen would apply. However, if this approach were used in group work, members would need to be directly oriented to the framework. In such an orientation, the therapist might need to provide illustrations and examples about appropriate responses and demeanor.

Conducting one-to-one interviews with individuals or couples, having the other group members share reflections, and then allowing the focal members to reflect on the reflections may take quite a bit of time, and it might seem that there is a direct benefit only to the interviewee. However, the other group members could also benefit from learning the protocol as well as from applying their reflections to themselves and other relationships in their lives.

A variation on the reflecting team model that could be used in the context of a group or as a way of socializing group members into the approach would be for the therapist to reflect aloud after conducting a one-to-one interview with a group member. However, with this approach the therapist must make multiple observations rather than only one, for any single observation could be viewed as the true story rather than a reflection. Indeed, it may be useful in group work in general for leaders to augment their repertoire with multiple alternative stories and to learn to reflect positively, discreetly, respectfully, sensitively, imaginatively, tentatively or speculatively, and creatively.

# Therapeutic Conversations of Harlene Anderson and Harry Goolishian

Among the various names used to describe the approach of Anderson and Goolishian are "therapeutic conversation," "collaborative language systems," and "narrative therapy." Harlene Anderson and Harry Goolishian strove to move away from the interventionist, change-oriented instrumentalism of first-order cybernetics. As an alternative, they suggested that the therapist and client jointly create a series of caring, empathic, therapeutic conversations. As Anderson (1993, p. 324) noted, "The therapists' pre-experiences and pre-knowledges do not lead. In this process both the therapist's and the client's expertise are engaged to dissolve problems." Further, the aim is to minimize "the consciousness of the therapist in pushing for, strategizing about, or designing the form of a therapeutic outcome" (Becvar & Becvar, 1996, p. 288).

Anderson and Goolishian believe that one's sense of self and one's problems are socially constructed; that is, they are created in conversations and embedded in language. In other words, one needs to have a concept or construct in order to have a conversation about it, but once the conversation about a problem metaphor begins, it choreographs relationships for continuing conversations about the metaphor. Thus, the concept or construct of "depression" is a key to the kinds of dialogues that may ensue between a traditional therapist and a client or between family members and the dialogues that keep the concept alive. There is no news of difference if the concept is believed to be a real thing; that is, if a concept or construct is believed to be true or real, this precludes alternative stories.

Challenging the first-order cybernetics notion that the system creates the problem, Anderson and Goolishian contended that the problem, as a consensually validated, objectified pathology, creates the system (Hoffman, 1993). The system thus organizes itself and maintains itself through conversations about the problem, which limits the kinds of conversations that are possible. Such conversations serve not only to maintain the problem but also to reify the metaphor.

The purpose of therapeutic conversations is to evolve new meaning with clients. The focus is on creating a therapy that is "less hierarchical, more egalitarian, mutual, respectful, and human, a therapy which allows a therapist to be aware of the depth, existence, and experiences of the individual" (Anderson, 1992, p. 21). Therapists who use this model do not view themselves as experts and they value multiple perspectives. That is, "The therapist's knowledge, experience and values are no truer than the client's—nor more final" (Hoffman-Hennessay & Davis, 1993, p. 343). Goolishian described the process as follows:

In the therapy room I am a learner. I adopt a "puzzling" position. This flips the position of the client and therapist. The client is now the knower, and the therapist is the not knower.... It is not just the therapist trying to understand the client, collecting information and data and placing [them] on some kind of cognitive map in a unilateral way. Rather, it is a mutual search in which client and therapist puzzle together in search for understanding, to develop a story that has not been told before. (quoted in Winderman, 1989, p. 1)

Goolishian (1991) elaborated further:

It is in the telling and retelling that the narrative changes. We think of the therapist as a participant narrative artist engaged in the co-construction of new meaning, new meaning and story that is coherent with the fragments of memory of the old stories. It is as if the therapist is a conversational participant, as opposed to being a narrative editor. (p. 1)

The general description we have presented provides about as clear an idea about what occurs in the therapeutic conversations as can be found. No formula exists. Indeed, there cannot be a formula, for each conversation is a unique, one-time experience that reflects the unique combination of people involved. What seems significant in this approach is that the process of the conversation is believed to be sufficient to make a difference; no grand intervention or definitive interpretation or assignment is relied on.

From reviewing a videotape of Goolishian's (1993) conversation or consultation with a blended family and a case report by Anderson (1993) about therapeutic work with a mother and daughter, we were, however, able to create categories or classes of interventions. From the Goolishian tape, our categories include (a) curious inquiry to allow multiple stories to emerge ("What kinds of things were you noticing that raised those issues and questions?"); (b) questions involving paraphrase or empathy to give rise to dialogue; such questions open up and expand the field of vision and may move outside the boundaries of the problem discourse ("So you go back and forth between your parents each week, and you get kind of mixed up about it?"); (c) questions that open up fresh dialogue and future possibilities, as well as other aspects or characteristics of individual family members ("Where did that musical talent come from?"); (d) questions followed by normalizing ("And what were you all fighting about? Just nothing? Fights go that way sometimes?"); (e) questions that are empowering ("How did you get calm so quickly?"); and (f) working to not understand too quickly, for to do so would shut down dialogue and suggest that a "final" story has been attained. Because many possible stories exist, "to understand" may shut down dialogue about additional possible stories. Other categories might include "walking with someone" through his or her story and asking questions to let multiple stories evolve. In general, the kinds of questions Goolishian asked aimed at keeping the dialogue open and evolving. In his view, there is no one right or "final" story, or the final story is that there is no final story.

From Harlene Anderson's (1993) report on a case involving a mother and a child who ran away frequently, we noted the following intervention categories: (a) inquiring about the problem; (b) being respectful and curious about the current "reality" of the clients; (c) asking questions and making comments empathically; and (d) offering positive connotations. One could infer that Anderson's goals might have included helping the clients feel heard and helping them to hear each other. In Anderson's words:

> Choices of questions, comments or other utterances by the therapist may limit the client's story because they may, implicitly or explicitly, convey a position, an agenda, or an expected response. I want to make choices that widen both my and the client's room for maneuverability, not narrow it. I want to demonstrate a "not knowing" position. I want to be a responsive active listener and to ask conversational questions.
>
> The immediate dialogic event, the developing narrative, informs the next question; the questions are not formed by the therapist's preconceived theories of what the story should be.... Each question, each utterance by the therapist, is an element of an overall process and comes from an honest, continuous therapeutic posture of not understanding too quickly, of not knowing. (1993, pp. 330–331)

# Applying Anderson and Goolishian's Approach to Group Work

How can a therapeutic conversation that is construed as a unique, one-time event and that cannot be formulaic be utilized in group work? Two possibilities come to mind. One is that one-to-one conversations could be conducted with each group member, with the other group members observing and possibly benefiting from the "modeling" of these unique, one-time-only conversations. The observers would likely look for pattern and consistency, and there is no doubt that they would find a pattern. Perhaps ultimately they might come to the conclusion that the pattern is that there is no pattern except that each conversation is a unique event. Randomness and uniqueness are the pattern. Undoubtedly, other patterns would also be inferred, for a limited range of behaviors exist that could legitimately be classified as constituting a caring, empathetic, nonhierarchical conversation. Further, the types of questions used by the therapist to understand current stories, to expand frames and help clients open up to the possibility of other stories, and to help group members hear one another and encourage future possibilities also might be seen as a pattern.

A second possibility would be to use Anderson and Goolishian's approach as a normative process in the group. The leader could give participants free rein to have conversations with one another, intervening, when requested, to help approximate the therapeutic conversations envisioned by the approach. Of course, the intervention by the leader would need to take the form of a conversation with each member about the conversation in which he or she took part. Rather than assuming Satir's corrective, expert stance, the leader would observe until the participants asked for assistance rather than interjecting and "correcting" a conversation according to a particular standard. To do otherwise would violate a fundamental assumption of the approach.

# Externalization and Reauthoring Lives and Relationships: White and Epston

In their adherence to the postmodernist position of Foucault, Michael White and David Epston (Epston, 1994; White, 1991; White & Epston, 1990) have offered a fundamental challenge to traditional mental health practice. They have asserted that "human science disciplines characterize, classify, distribute along a scale, around a norm, hierarchize individuals in relation to one another, and if necessary disqualify and invalidate" (White & Epston, 1990, p. 74). Thus, in their view, people's subjective experiences are objectified and their personal stories are subjugated, repressed, denied, and replaced by normative classification schemes that society and professional experts bill as the politically, psychologically, and socially correct ways for people to live their lives. In other words, as the normative psychology of a society permeates the thinking of the consumer, people watch themselves and others for the "warning signs of problems" and then engage in discourses about those warning signs, thereby creating the reality described by the normative standards. Accordingly, members of the society internalize the normative standards and the deficit-based, diagnostic categories, and consumers become an extension of traditional, normative, mental health practice. The process of normalization requires participation in the "compulsory objectification" of subjective experiences into "ultimate truth stories" that preclude the search for alternative stories outside their frame.

A key idea in the traditional, normative approach is the concept of internalization of a problem-saturated, ultimate truth story that a person holds about him- or herself and that other people in that person's life hold about the focal person. Thus, a first step for the postmodernist therapist when dealing with any kind of problem, in White and Epston's view, is to externalize or objectify the problem as a thing separate from the person. Through the process of externalization the therapist seeks to empower clients to rely on their own lived experience, "which falls outside the dominant stories about the lives and relationships of persons" (White & Epston, 1990, p. 15). In an elaboration of the assumption that drives their approach to therapy, White and Epston (1990) wrote:

> Stories are full of gaps which persons must fill in order for the stories to be performed. These gaps recruit the lived experience and the imagination of persons. With every performance, persons are reauthoring their lives. The evolution of lives is akin to their process of reauthoring, the process of persons' entering stories, taking them over and making them their own. (p. 13)

In other words, empowering clients to reauthor their own lives involves the process of deconstructing the universal truth stories that are living their lives for them. Externalization requires that the client separate him- or herself from the problem. Externalization also:

1. Decreases unproductive conflict between persons, including those disputes over who is responsible for the problem;
2. Undermines the sense of failure that has developed for many persons in response to the continuing existence of the problem despite their attempts to resolve it;
3. Paves the way for persons to cooperate with each other, to unite in a struggle against the problem, and to escape its influence in their lives and relationships;
4. Opens up new possibilities for persons to take action to retrieve their lives and relationships from the problem and its influence;
5. Frees persons to take a lighter, more effective, and less stressed approach to "deadly serious" problems; and
6. Presents options for dialogue, rather than monologue, about the problem. (White & Epston, 1990, pp. 39–40)

Like most postmodernists, White and Epston use various kinds of questioning. Externalization questions—such as, "How has the problem affected your life?"—require answers that objectify the problem and locate it outside the person for examination. Relative-influence questions—such as, "How has the problem (not the person) influenced your life and your relationships with others?" and "What influence have you had on the life of the problem?"—require that people move away from their vision of a "fixed and static world, a world of problems that are intrinsic to persons and relationships, and into a world of experience, a world of flux" (White & Epston, 1990, p. 42).

In addition, "unique-outcome" questions ask for instances that represent lived experience outside the problem-saturated, universal truth story. For example, the therapist might ask, "Would you describe a time when depression did not keep you from doing what you wanted to do?" Please note that the question, "Have there been any times when depression did not keep you from doing what you wanted to do?" does not work to this end. Followers of White and Epston's approach assume that nothing is always or never. Gaps in people's problem-saturated stories exist. The questions are keyed to "when" rather than "if" these experiences occurred. Further, the therapist does not dismiss small events in the client's response as being too trivial. Each response illustrating an example represents an opening. However, these previously unarticulated facts of lived experience must be significant enough or frequent enough to challenge the validity of the totalizing pathology story, especially if the diagnosis has been made by a mental health professional. If a series of unique outcomes, however small and seemingly insignificant, are articulated, the negative story can be challenged, for empowerment and personal agency are implied.

Unique outcomes represent alternative stories that the client must take into account if he or she is to experience a coherent life story. Thus, the client must integrate such reports into his or her lived experience. As persons become the audience for their own performance of these alternative stories, which clients can repeat or enlarge upon, they can begin to become the authors of their own lives and to create new stories about their lived experience. It is important that unique-outcome questions solicit stories from both recent and distant history; the range gives them more credibility in the face of the cultural pathology story they are intended to displace.

White (1995, p. 65) reported that at first "these alternative stories of identity are 'thin' and, as well, they do not seem very sustainable." To help these stories become "thick" or "'rich,' descriptions of a person's life and history," he asks what might be called "external validation" questions (our metaphor). White provided some examples of these questions:

> I have the beginning of some understanding of how you survived this, and of some of the skills and personal qualities that you have relied upon to get you through this time. Can you think of anyone who has known you who might have been in touch with this other story of your life that is becoming more visible in this work?" Or, "I am developing some appreciation of the constructive steps that you have recently taken in your project to break from self-rejection. In your entire life, can you think of anyone who has known you who wouldn't be surprised to hear of these recent constructive developments in your life?" (p. 65)

These significant others can be invited to participate in the therapy sessions to help the client "re-member" incidents that are evidence of alternative stories in the person's life.

White and Epston designated another set of questions as "experience-of-experience" questions, for they encourage persons to provide an account of what they believe or imagine to be another person's experience of them. Questions include: "How do you think my knowing this has affected my view of you as a person?" and "Are there other people in your life who have noted these facts of your experience?"

From White and Epston's perspective, the questions they ask and the assumptions they make are illustrative rather than prescriptive. Each conversation is unique rather than formulaic. And sometimes far more important than the questions are the answers, which may cue more fruitful questions. Indeed, in the process of therapy, White and Epston seem interested in educating people about what they believe to be the storied nature of their human experience. They value people learning to not automatically defer to normative stories and being able to utilize what they have learned in therapy in their future lives.

# Applying White and Epston's Approach to Group Work

In our judgment, the greatest challenge in applying White and Epston's approach to group therapy is the inevitable establishment in a group of a normative group process, something that is implicit in the concept "group." Postmodernists try to be nonnormative. The paradox, of course, is that in attempting to be nonnormative, one creates an alternative set of norms relative to solving human dilemmas and problems.

However, as with the other postmodern approaches, one-to-one therapy in a group following White and Epston's approach would seem workable. Other group members, acting as observers of the focal group member and the leader, would learn the process of the dialogue and questioning, the "rules" implicit in White and Epston's approach. They might apply these rules to themselves even before taking a turn as the focal person. As they internalize these rules, or process goals, they also might have conversations with one another in the spirit of the approach.

In addition, it would seem consistent with White and Epston's approach to do "therapy in groups," that is, to teach consumers as well as therapists the subject matter and the process of their approach to problem solving. White (1995) described how his approach could be used in conversations with teachers and students in a school setting. Further, an exercise he presented, developed by Sallyann Roth and David Epston to help people explore externalizing conversations, could be applicable in a variety of settings including therapy in groups. The conversations within groups would focus on the discussion of the subject matter and participants would apply the subject matter and the process of White and Epston's approach to their lives in the same way that trained therapists apply the subject matter and process to their work as therapists. Thus, deliberate psychological education would focus on deconstructing problem-saturated stories (diagnostic metaphors) consistent with traditional, normative, mental health practice. Through the conversations, group members could reauthor their own lives and create their own personal psychology in their own language.

Laube and Trefz (1994) described an application of White and Epston's narrative approach in group therapy for depression. For their application, the group can be open-ended or closed. Its focus is on member collaboration, members' narratives, and externalization of problem-saturated stories. The group leader and members, according to Laube and Trefz,

> become audience and collaborators who bring forth stories of lived experience. Together they create an environment where people can listen and be heard without critique or editing. Gradually, the group interaction creates emotional space by enlarging the story of depression to include tales of survival, resistance, and creativity. (p. 31)

In the process, the members develop a story of themselves that evolves over the life of the group, and each member develops a story about his or her place in the group story. Members become self-conscious of living their lives in stories and creating stories. Further, Laube and Trefz stated, "the language of the group is infused with familiar words that are used in narrating and reading and creating stories: character, point of view, plot, development, action, story line, climax, voice, setting, style, tragedy, farce scene, chapter, page, perspective, etc." (1994, p. 34).

Finally, in applications of White and Epston's approach to group work, the group members might serve as a reflecting team. The team would indicate appreciation of the focal member's situation and respond to unique outcomes or preferred happenings with curiosity, asking questions such as, "How did you manage to take this important step?" As with Tom Andersen's reflecting team approach, however, team members would be instructed to not offer moral stories or homilies.

Adams-Westcott and Isenbart (1996) described a model applying the narrative approach to groups of individuals and couples recovering from child sexual abuse. Given that an important part of the process of externalization and reauthoring lives involves challenging "the sociopolitical conditions that contribute to violence and victimization," their model focuses on "the ways in which cultural stories about gender roles and expectations, power, intimacy, and sexuality contribute to personal stories about victimization" (p. 13).

Unlike the more traditional therapy models that construe the experience of child sexual abuse as baggage clients must carry with them throughout their lives, Adams-Westcott and Isenbart used White and Epston's "rites of passage analogy" according to which "symptoms and crises are considered evidence of progress, and indicate that the person has already begun separating from a story that is no longer viable" (Adams-Westcott & Isenbart, 1996, p. 14). In their work, the individual is the primary focus of the therapy, but they believe that group members can make important contributions by using "perspectives that are not colored by [an] 'abuse-dominated lens'" (p. 14).

An important aspect of this model involves helping group members become consciously aware of the sociopolitical discourses (i.e., gender beliefs and practices, sexuality, intimacy, power) that maintain the experience described by these discourses and focusing the conversations with group members on "re-sources" and on creating preferred futures. The authors described specific questions and activities that can be used with both the person who experienced childhood sexual abuse and the partner of that person. Both partners learn about and externalize the focal person's story. They look for unique outcomes and begin to restory their individual lives and their lives together.

Roth and Epston (1996) described an exercise for helping people develop externalizing conversations. This exercise, for groups of six people, could be used in training as well as in therapy. In the latter setting, it provides clients with an experience of a narrative focus, enabling them to learn from both their own and the therapist's perspectives the effects of the various kinds of questions associated with White and Epston's approach. Specific components include:

    I. Setting up the exercise
    II. Interviewing the problem
        A. The influence of the problem on persons
            1. Plainly put questions about the modes and degree of this influence

2. Imagistically rich question about modes and degree of the influence of the problem on persons

3. Imagistically rich hypothetical questions about the future influence of the problem on persons

III. Free-flowing inquiry

IV. Reflections on what has happened (Roth & Epston, 1996, pp. 6–12)

Alice Morgan (1995) describes another application of White and Epston's approach in group consultation with students who bully and tease other students. Rather than psychologizing about and developing professionally engineered programs for the problem, she consulted with perpetrators "who were quite surprised to be asked" (p. 22). Morgan notes that many schools seek to help students develop coping skills to deal with others who bully and tease. She writes, "To ask victims of the abuse to spell out the effects of that abuse on their lives is to heap one injustice upon another, and further burdens the victim" (p. 19).

Morgan believes the goal of reducing the incidence of bullying and teasing could best be accomplished "if the abuse perpetrators accepted full responsibility for their abusive actions" (p. 19). Her approach involved getting the perpetrators together to speak in their own voices against the abuse instead of relying on the voices of those who were subjected to it.

In addition to a respectful, not knowing attitude, three guiding principles orient her work with the students:

- Declining explicit invitations to attribute responsibility for teasing to factors beyond the students' influence, whilst inviting them to take responsibility for their teasing.
- Inviting the students to challenge restraints to acceptance of responsibility.
- Acknowledging and highlighting evidence of the students' accepting responsibility for their actions. (pp. 19–20)

Her approach would seem to be a good fit with other problems in schools and other contexts. Another applications of this approach with abuse and men who are violent is described by Jenkins (1990).

# Solution-Oriented Therapy: Steve de Shazer and Insoo Berg

Steve de Shazer and his wife and colleague, Insoo Berg (Berg & de Shazer, 1993; de Shazer, 1984, 1985, 1991, 1994), created an approach, built on the work of Wittgenstein and Derrida, that essentially deconstructs traditional problem solving methods in therapy. They contend that one does "not need to know what the problem is in order to solve it," that "the problem or complaint is not necessarily related to the solution," and that "the solution is not necessarily related to the problem" (de Shazer, 1991, p. xiii). In fact, they do not speculate about how any approach works, for, as they stated, "One can only know that it does work" (de Shazer, 1991, p. xviii).

Their approach appears to have been influenced by both the work of Milton Erickson and de Shazer's early training at MRI, where the assumption is that the attempted solution is the problem. De Shazer and Berg take the position that attempting to solve a problem in ineffective ways or, indeed, attempting to solve the problem at all serves to maintain it. In therapy, ineffective ways to solve the problem include conversations about the problem and extensive history-taking aimed at seeking causal processes. Thus, in their approach, talk about the problem is minimal. Rather, the focus is on helping clients learn a new connection between problem and solution, that is, helping clients to see that there is no "real" problem. Indeed, one could say from this perspective that clients enter therapy not knowing how to get where they want to go and the therapy is designed to help them get there. Getting rid of the problem does not necessarily mean they will get where they want to go.

De Shazer and Berg's approach is nonnormative. It is respectful of the unique emotional system that is each client, and, as such, solutions must be tailor-made for each client. It is also a complaint-based approach. When clients no longer experience the complaint that brought them to therapy, the therapy is finished. In addition, de Shazer and Berg speak of narratives and life stories rather than of reality. They believe that all stories have beginnings, middles, ends, and plots and that all stories deal with human dilemmas, solutions, and attempted solutions. Borrowing an idea from Gergen and Gergen (1986), they described three kinds of narratives (de Shazer, 1991, p. 92):

1. Progressive narratives that justify the conclusion that people and situations are progressing toward their goals.
2. Stability narratives that justify the conclusion that life is unchanging.
3. Digressive narratives that justify the conclusion that life is moving away from goals.

De Shazer and Berg view progressive narratives as the most useful type and contrasted them with complaint-centered narratives (stability or digressive narratives), which they feel are the usual form of therapeutic story construction. In their view, the goals for therapy should be the articulation of statements about what will be present in the client's life. An important question that can be used to help clients articulate their goals is the "miracle question":

> Suppose that one night there is a miracle, and while you were sleeping the problem that brought you to therapy is solved. How would you know? What would be different?
> What will you notice different the next morning that will tell you that there has been a miracle? What will your spouse notice? (de Shazer, 1991, p. 112)

Further, they view goals for therapy as useful if they are:

1. Small rather than large
2. Salient to clients
3. Described in specific, concrete, behavioral terms
4. Achievable within the practical context of clients' lives
5. Perceived by the clients as involving their "hard work"
6. Described as the "start of something" and not as the "end of something"
7. Treated as involving new behavior(s) rather than the absence or cessation of existing behavior(s) (de Shazer, 1991, p. 112)

The approach also has an important focus on language. That is, therapy is viewed as a language game involving shared meanings. In therapy, meanings are shared as a means of moving from problem $X$ (problem-talk and getting rid of the problem) to problem $Y$ (talk about solutions and about moving toward goals). The only meaning of a word that is important and possible is the meaning that participants have assigned to it in a conversation about the word. The question, "How do you know you are depressed?" seeks information about, and seeks to create self-awareness of, the experiences in the client's life that have led him or her to assign the metaphor "depression" to him- or herself. A more direct and yet similar question that has a clear constructivist perspective might be, "What are your criteria for assigning the metaphor depression to yourself?" The client's definition of the metaphor "depressed" provides information about how the therapist and client participate in reconstructing or restorying the client's experience. The process of questioning about the story involves cocreating a normal difficulty rather than a pathological problem having roots in infancy. The client's goals and solutions thus are more important than the problem depicted in the client's narrative.

In their discussions of language, de Shazer and Berg talk of the process of "creatively misunderstanding." De Shazer (1991, p. 69) wrote, "Following the second law of thermodynamics, misunderstanding (chaos) is much more likely than understanding (order)." Thus, in creatively misunderstanding, therapists use language to help clients "construct a reality that is more satisfactory" (p. 69). De Shazer and Berg also see the language game of therapy as allowing for "binocular vision," or depth perception, where the different descriptions on the part of the people in a conversation are put together to create new meaning. If a team of observers is used, de Shazer and Berg talk of "polyocular" vision, reminding the reader that different descriptions must not be too different.

With this approach, once goals are established, the therapist asks questions or solicits information that fosters an inversion to solutions. Clients become aware that nothing is always or never and that "exceptions" always exist. Thus, an intervention aimed at inverting a conversation toward talk about solutions might include the request, "Tell me about the times, however few, when you feel okay or good, when you do accomplish things, enjoy your friends, etc." The difference between that request and the question, "Do you ever feel okay or good about yourself, accomplish things, or enjoy your friends?" describes the difference between *when* and *if*. The therapist assumes that clients are doing some things that work some of the time. The search for and articulation of exceptions serve to deconstruct the totalizing experience of the complaint. The process also plants the seed that the client already is exerting some control over the complaint. Follow-up questions can serve to empower. The therapist might ask, for example,

"How did you do that?" or "How did you two manage to have an okay day on Saturday?" In a variation on the search for exceptions, the therapist can ask questions (to be answered in the session or as a homework assignment) about things happening in a client's life that he or she would like to continue. Such questions can lead to discussions about the fact that as clients move toward their goals, they may want to be sure they do not give up some important things.

Some interventions in de Shazer and Berg's approach are used to help clients develop progressive narratives. For example, the therapist might ask, "What is better now?" or "What did you do well this week?" rather than "How did your week go?" or "Were things better this week?" The former questions plant the seed that better things have happened and focus a client's attention on the good things that occur in all lives.

De Shazer and Berg also use scaling questions, which assess the client's perception of degrees of change experienced, to help clients develop progressive narratives. They might ask, for example, "On a scale of 0 to 10, with 10 representing your experience when your depression is gone and 0 representing how you felt when you called for an appointment, where would you place how you feel at this time?" They describe another intervention they use as "cheerleading" (de Shazer, 1991), whereby the therapist acknowledges and celebrates the client's movement toward his or her goals as well as any increase in the frequency of exceptions to the experience of a problem. Empowering questions like "How did you do that?" would complement cheerleading. Encouragement can be offered in the form of "Keep doing more of what is working for you."

As we close this brief summary of the solution-oriented perspective of de Shazer and Berg, we acknowledge the wealth of ideas for solution-oriented therapy that could be gleaned from other therapists, such as, Eve Lipchik (Lipchik & de Shazer, 1986; O'Hanlon, 1993; O'Hanlon & Weiner-Davis, 1989; Walter & Peller, 1992). Our focus on de Shazer and Berg was somewhat arbitrary. However, their approach appears to be more consistent with the second-order cybernetics/constructivist and social constructionist perspectives than others are.

# Applying de Shazer and Berg's Approach to Group Work

As with all the postmodernist approaches, inconsistencies are involved in applying the ideas of de Shazer and Berg to group work. The primary inconsistency is that simply by bringing into the picture group therapy, in which a normative process is facilitated, and leader facilitation results in socialization into that normative process. Even so, like White and Epston's approach, de Shazer and Berg's deconstruction and constructionist approach to problem solving could be taught to consumers in much the same way it is taught to therapists. Again, the process is one of deliberate psychological education about problem solving and how traditional ways of problem solving may be participating in creating and maintaining problems. Such teaching would fit our definition of therapy in groups, but it would not fit what we define as group therapy unless the agenda is made explicit up front and disclaimers made about this not being the only way to solve problems (see Atkinson, 1992, whose thoughts on the matter were articulated earlier in this chapter). An excellent paper by Coe and Zimpfer (in press), to be published in the *Journal for Specialists in Group Work*, articulates a general, solution-oriented approach and how it could play out in group counseling.

We believe that de Shazer and Berg's approach could be used in one-to-one work in a group context. Group members observing the process could learn the approach vicariously in addition to what they learn in their own personal work with the therapist. Some solution-oriented group dialogue could be facilitated when members have become sufficiently familiar with the approach.

Selekman (1991) describes a solution-focused parenting group that involves psychoeducation. Specifically, parents in the group are taught the basic philosophy and principles of solution-focused therapy. Consistent with these principles, parents are encouraged and encourage each other to look for exceptions to problem behavior, notice small changes and become aware of what they have done to promote the changes (self-consciously or not), do more of what is working, do something different if what they are doing is not working, building on and celebrating small successes. Group discussion and support by group members is continuous throughout the life of the group.

# In Conclusion

The brief reviews of second-order cybernetic/constructivist and so-cial constructionist approaches to therapy presented in this chapter as well as the ideas we presented about their application to group work obviously are not exhaustive. However, our intent was merely to dem-onstrate how, with further study, some of the ideas underlying these models might be useful in group work. We are aware, of course, that with their particular philosophical orientation, which challenges the searches for universal principles and the creation of totalizing dis-courses at the pragmatic level, postmodernists face the dilemma of offering metauniversal principles and metatotalizing discourses. We discussed this paradox of self-reference at the end of Chapter 2. It also is one of several issues we discuss in Chapter 7.

# 7

# Epistemological, Ethical, and Evaluation Issues

*I*n this chapter we explore a variety of issues that evolved for us as we wrote this book. Some of these issues concern epistemology. Some are ethical. Some involve evaluation and research.

## Epistemological Issues

Our attempts to fit first-order cybernetics, second-order cybernetics, constructivism, and social constructionism to various forms of group work raised a variety of epistemological issues. Some of those issues came to the fore in what we refer to as the paradigm shift to a first-order cybernetic perspective. Other epistemological issues arose when we explored the contrasting philosophical traditions of modernism and postmodernism and considered second-order cybernetics, constructivism, and social constructionism. Our major question concerned whether or not models or approaches consistent with these frameworks fit group work.

From our discussions we concluded that our answer to the question regarding fit is a qualified "yes." All three of us adhere to the fundamental assumption that any form of thinking can be useful in any therapeutic context. However, we also believe that each theory, model, or approach should be examined for consistency within itself rather than being compared to or judged from assumptions that derive from another theory, model, or approach. Thus, when we applied models and approaches from first- and second-order cybernetics, constructivism, and social constructionism to group work, we tried to stay within or be logically consistent with the assumptions of each model or approach. Our conclusion was that some, but not all, models or approaches from these perspectives fit some forms of group work. And the fit seemed most tenuous when we attempted to think about doing group work from the perspectives of second-order cybernetics/constructivism and social constructionism.

Throughout this book we have mentioned a variety of challenges that these perspectives present to traditional mental health practice. First-order cybernetics challenges the basic unit of analysis valued by Western societies: the individual or the monad. Recall Watzlawick's (1990) statement quoted in Chapter 1 regarding how therapists following the first-order cybernetic perspective, must shift to seeing disturbed relationships rather than disturbed individuals. However, although this shift is significant, it stays within the modernist framework of the observer independent of the observed and continues to assume, like the modernist perspective that one can observe without intruding. Still included in first-order cybernetics approaches is the possibility of making objective assessments of a system. Further, therapists continue to see individuals as functional in social contexts and relationships as dysfunctional or disturbed. From this framework, the system is the logical unit of analysis and is the focus of treatment for "disturbed" individuals.

Second-order cybernetics represents an even greater epistemological challenge to modernist thought with its introduction of the concept of participant-observer. The observer must include himself or herself in the system he or she is "observing" and must recognize that he or she participates in creating the reality experienced. In this shift to a constructivist perspective, the participant-observer becomes aware that believing is seeing rather than seeing is believing. In other words, if one thinks and acts in a way logically consistent with a particular framework, the unit under "observation" takes on the form of that belief. The world in which such individuals live and work is one of personal construction rather than a world of facts. This shift in thinking influences not only mental health practice but also the conception of knowledge. Although second-order cybernetics does not preclude thinking in terms of adaptive or maladaptive individuals or systems, the therapist is consciously aware of the implications of the stories he or she chooses to focus on in discussions of the life of the individual or system.

Perhaps the greatest epistemological challenge to modernist mental health practice and group work comes from social constructionism combined with second-order cybernetics/constructivism. From these perspectives, the therapist is no longer the expert with final, privileged knowledge. The therapeutic context is conversational. Therapists consciously try to be nonpathologizing, nonobjectifying, noncontrolling, curious, nonhierarchical, and respectful. Moreover, the therapist focuses on the client's socially constructed story rather than on either the person or a system.

The perspectives of second-order cybernetics/constructivism and social constructionism suggest that any form of therapy provides a context that is constructed to transform human experiences and related behavior, which also are constructions. So, those who adhere to these perspectives construct contexts for transforming constructions. The formal study of the therapy process can thus be described as constructing concepts for effectively constructing therapy contexts. Therapists are floating in the semantic space of a world that is all made up. Knowledge is value, and framework relative.

It seems appropriate to consider this issue of context in a discourse about the concept "group" and the varying forms of group work. Groups can be viewed as contexts in which people learn the ecology of ideas that orients their thinking about themselves and influences the development of their identities, as well as their thinking about their thinking. Groups also can be viewed as contexts that expect of members, and enforce, specific forms of political, social, and psychological correctness. Groups are powerful, and group work in any of its forms can be powerful. Its power must be respected. Because a group is a miniature society, group work has the power to alleviate pain and suffering, or it can be toxic. It can solve problems at one level while creating higher-order problems. And thus we move our discussion into the realm of ethics.

# Ethical Issues

Most professional codes of ethics orient professional practice at the level of first-order cybernetics. Thus, group leaders are constrained to work within a particular conceptual framework of legal and ethical practice. The group leader's roles are defined, and he or she is accountable for practice consistent with this framework. The appropriateness or inappropriateness of any group leader behavior is based on the value consensus of professional peers and the larger society. From this perspective, any form of group work requires an awareness of and adherence to certain behaviors defined as ethical and establishes boundaries that cannot be breached without risk of professional sanctions. Such role expectations and boundaries serve to protect the profession and to safeguard the welfare of clients.

The responsibilities of group facilitation therefore are based on the ethical and legal imperatives of society as stipulated in various laws and ethical codes of conduct. Specific day-to-day responsibilities of mental health professionals may vary according to jurisdiction and political climate, but the basic ethical responsibilities of all therapists remain constant and stem from the philosophical concept of beneficence. This concept requires that the therapist provide assistance and in the process do no harm. Moreover, societal standards define "who may do what to whom," as well as the parameters in which what is done may be done. As such, there are responsibilities to which group leaders must adhere regardless of theoretical orientation, worldview, or epistemology.

These responsibilities of group facilitation include establishing the broad parameters of the purpose of the group, membership selection criteria, and a variety of basic group structural components, such as size, duration, frequency of meetings, and so forth. Additionally, the group facilitator has the responsibility to safeguard and protect all group members from unjustifiable or unreasonable physical and psychological distress.

Although group leaders working from the perspectives of second-order cybernetics/constructivism or social constructionism must adhere to the codes of ethics for first-order cybernetic professional practice, they may view professional practice as prescribed for the practice of first-order group work as unethical. That is, from these postmodern perspectives, professional mental health practice and group work in the tradition of modernism participates in creating the problems that they ultimately "treat." As noted in the introduction to Chapter 6, whereas a first-order cybernetician attempts to understand what is "really" going on or what the "real" problem is, the second-order cybernetician views himself or herself as a participant in creating reality (Keeney, 1982, p. 165). This difference in perspective makes a world of difference.

Thus, a second-order ethic comes into play for which there is no formal code to guide professional practice. Nor should there be, for therapists working from a second-order cybernetics perspective consider codes of ethics at the level of first-order cybernetics to be social constructions that are logically consistent with the socially constructed ideas that participate in creating pathology. Thus, the very act of doing first-order professional practice raises second-order ethical questions. Accordingly, as a participant-observer and a person who believes that knowledge is a social construction, the second-order cybernetic therapist considers it unethical to represent him- or herself as an expert with definitive final knowledge. The therapist also considers it unethical to pathologize, objectify, control, diagnose, and be hierarchical in his or her professional practice. For second-order therapists, ethical issues in group work therefore may involve the following:

- Discerning (creating) a "need" or "problem" that may define the purpose of the group
- Deciding that the group context is a better context in which to serve a particular purpose than other experiences might be
- Selecting members for the group and informing members of the advantages and risks they may experience by their participation
- Selecting a theoretical model and related process goals to guide therapeutic discourse in the group
- Being aware of the possibility of creating more serious problems by attempting to meet the need or solve the problem that defines the purpose of the group; included here are questions about the goodness of fit for people who are ethnically, racially, or culturally different from the majority population as well as for women and people of a sexual orientation different from that of the majority

- Being aware of how change in group members may affect other people in the group members' natural contexts
- Being aware of the possibility of reifying the metaphor describing the "need" or problem

From a second-order ethical position, the first-order process of diagnosing (assigning a DSM deficit label to an individual or even a relational diagnosis to a couple or family), formulating a treatment plan based on that diagnosis, and treating the problem is problematic. A related issue that forms a fundamental paradox second-order therapists and group leaders must face is that they are asked to fix that which is not broken when viewed from within the larger social context and its ecology of ideas. What is more, therapists' awareness of this paradox may be one of the main reasons why systemic, cybernetic, constructivist, and social constructionist perspectives remain peripheral to mainstream mental health practice. We described the dilemma postmodern therapists face elsewhere:

> Indeed, one can infer from the higher-order systems model that if societies had evolved paradigms and processes consistent with the ideals set forth by those societies, then therapy per se would not be a role in the society. A society evolves the role of therapist to deal with discrepancies between its ideals and the processes based on it, which the society activates to attain these ideals. (Becvar & Becvar, 1996, p. 364)

Others also have described this dilemma of working between the two philosophical extremes of modernism and postmodernism. For example, Stewart and Amundson (1995, p. 71) stated:

> While we may find value in adopting the notion that truth is relative in order to avoid the "final solutions" of modernism (Amundson, Stewart, & Perry, 1994), we are still left with the contingencies that our codes of ethics represent. These ethical principles prescribe the boundaries of our professional behavior, they tell us who is and who isn't a member of a given profession. They represent "certainties" we might not so easily deconstruct. While we may abandon the "truth" of theories that underlie the discourse of our profession, we cannot abandon the "final vocabularies" (Rorty, 1989) of our ethical principles themselves.

Thus, postmodernist therapists are faced with the ongoing dilemma of reconciling these two very different worldviews. This issue exists not only in the realm of ethics, but also in the related realm of evaluation and research. We consider such concerns next as they relate to group work.

# Evaluation and Research Issues

In the modernist perspective, where observer is separate from the system, evaluation and research are business as usual. That is, the formal assessment of the progress of group members from the perspective of the leader as expert is logically consistent. Empirical research in the spirit of logical positivism is also consistent and expected. Therapists can observe without intruding, and they can make controlled observations of phenomena "out there." In addition, if one is to diagnose, formulate a treatment plan, and treat from a standard therapy protocol, then the results obtained should be predictable. Hence, validity as well as reliability of such protocols are required in the development of standards for therapeutic interventions for real problems. Knowledge derived from these assessment and research protocols are viewed from the modernist and first-order perspective as "objective." Indeed, it is an ethical imperative ("first-order" ethics) that therapists formally evaluate and conduct research.

However, from the perspectives of second-order cybernetics/ constructivism and social constructionism, such first-order assessment and research protocols would be inconsistent and unethical ("second-order" ethics). Laird (1995) made the following observations regarding evaluation from a social constructionist perspective:

> If, in a social constructionist stance, neither science nor a search for "truth" undergird our efforts, to what are we held accountable? How do we evaluate our work? Are we left with a rampant relativism in which every "truth," every story, every intervention is equal? Clearly we need a new set of criteria for making judgments. But those criteria must account for the fact that we are valuing, meaning-making human beings, that none of us has an edge on truth, and that our values and meanings are always part of the reality that we are trying to understand.
>
> Accountability requires more than documentation of process and/or outcome. It also requires striving for practice that is moral, ethical, responsible, and just, in which the worker struggles to understand whose morality, whose justice, and whose meanings are being endorsed. As family theorist Keeney (1983) suggested, we must move from an ethic of objectivity to an ethic of responsibility. (p. 159)

When one moves from the position of expert operating from a hierarchical, independent-observer perspective to one of participant-observer collaborating with and empowering group members, the judgment about attaining what the group members came for rests solely with the group members. This process respects and empowers clients to be responsible for their values, beliefs, and actions.

Thus, even standardized, self-report questionnaires that include specific items (with or without scaling) could not be utilized, for such instruments impose a framework of values upon group members and necessarily restrict their response options. Open-ended oral or written reports of progress or lack thereof could be solicited from group members if the group leader were not the administrator. At the same time, the idea that the administrator be a different person from the group leader implies "objectivity," a posture that is inconsistent with the concept of therapy, evaluation, and research as a collaborative process. Morris, Gawinski, and Joanning (1994) described this dilemma as follows:

> The therapist and researcher are thus recursively connected in a pattern that undoes the heretofore positivist-based distinction which required their separation. The therapeutic-research endeavor becomes more involved with curiosity—a curiosity about how we all (including therapist and researcher) co-participate in the conversational creation of new meaning and new action. (p. 27)

We would add that group members also should be active coparticipants "in the conversational creation of new meaning and new action," if therapists are to be consistent with second-order cybernetics/ constructivism and social constructionism. No less is required if respect for and the empowerment of clients is what therapists are about.

# In Conclusion

As a final note, we wish to remind you that this book, of course, is our construction and should not be regarded as the final word on any of the topics addressed. Rather, we hope that we have provided sufficient information to stimulate dialogue on the conceptual fit and the utility of first-order cybernetics, second-order cybernetics, constructivism, and social constructionism relative to group work.

For cyberneticians, constructivists, and social constructionists who embrace the perspectives to which we adhere, do not search for truth in an absolute sense. They assume that a God's-eye view of the world will never be available to them. Thus, they search for stories that are more just and more fair, particularly for the marginalized people in their society. They are aided in their search for stories by being aware of the way in which their narratives are influenced and constrained by the societies and cultures to which they necessarily belong and that legitimate their roles as mental health professionals. Laird (1995, p. 160) noted that "therapy, for lack of a better term, should be in part a matter of deconstruction, of consciousness-raising, of learning how one's own stories have been constrained or demeaned or deprivileged in varying contexts of knowledge and power." In this spirit, we, as mental health professionals, believe that we must conduct an epistemological therapy on the received-view concepts that may not be serving us well. Doing so is not common in natural groups, therapy groups, or in professional groups. Nevertheless, we hope our efforts in this book are a contribution to that end.

# References

Adams-Westcott, J., & Isenbart, D. (1996). Creating preferred relationships: The politics of recovery from child sexual abuse. *Journal of Systemic Therapies, 15,* 13–30.

Amatea, E., & Sherrard, P. (1994). The ecosystemic view: A choice of lenses. *Journal of Mental Health Counseling, 16,* 6–21.

American Psychiatric Association. (1994). *Diagnostic and statistical manual of mental disorders* (4th ed., rev.). Washington, DC: Author.

Amundson, J., Stewart, K., & Perry, A. (1994). Whither narrative? The danger of getting it right. *Journal of Marital and Family Therapy, 20,* 83–88.

Andersen, T. (1987). The reflecting team: Dialogue and meta-dialogue in clinical work. *Family Process, 26,* 415–428.

Andersen, T. (Ed.). (1991). *The reflecting team: Dialogues and dialogues about the dialogues.* New York: W. W. Norton.

Andersen, T. (1992). Reflections on reflecting with families. In S. McNamee & K. J. Gergen (Eds.), *Therapy as social construction* (pp. 54–68). Newbury Park, CA: Sage.

Andersen, T. (1993). See and hear: And be seen and heard. In S. Friedman (Ed.), *The new language of change* (pp. 54–68). New York: Guilford.

Anderson, H. (1993). On a roller coaster: A collaborative language systems approach to therapy. In S. Friedman (Ed.), *The new language of change* (pp. 323–344). New York: Guilford.

Anderson, H., & Goolishian, H. (1988). Human systems as linguistic systems: Preliminary and evolving ideas about the implications for clinical theory. *Family Process, 27,* 271–293.

Anderson, H., & Goolishian, H. (1992). The client is the expert: A not-knowing approach to therapy. In S. McNamee & K. J. Gergen (Eds.), *Therapy as social construction* (pp. 25–39). Newbury Park, CA: Sage.

Atkinson, B. J. (1992). Aesthetics and pragmatics of family therapy revisited. *Journal of Marital and Family Therapy, 18,* 389–393.

Atkinson, B., & Heath, A. (1990a). Further thoughts on second-order family therapy—this time it's personal. *Family Process, 29,* 145–155.

Atkinson, B., & Heath, A. (1990b). The limits of explanation and evaluation. *Family Process, 29,* 164–167.

Bartlett, S. (1983). *Conceptual therapy: An introduction to framework—relative epis-temology.* St. Louis, MO: Crescere.

Bateson, G. (1972). *Steps to an ecology of mind.* New York: Ballantine.

Becker, H. S. (1967). Whose side are we on? In W. J. Filstead (Ed.), *Qualitative methodology: Firsthand involvement with the social world* (pp. 239–247). Chicago: Markham.

Becvar, D. S., & Becvar, R. J. (1994). *Hot chocolate for a cold winter night.* Denver: Love.

Becvar, D. S., & Becvar, R. J. (1996). *Family therapy: A systemic integration* (3rd ed.). Boston: Allyn & Bacon.

Becvar, R. & Becvar, D. (In Press). Comparing 2nd-order family therapy and Rogerian theory. *Journal of Systemic Therapies.*

Berg, I. K., & de Shazer, S. (1993). Making numbers talk: A solution-focused approach. In S. Friedman (Ed.), *The new language of change* (pp. 5–24). New York: Guilford.

Bergin, A. E. (1963). The effects of psychotherapy: Negative effects revisited. *Journal of Counseling Psychology, 10,* 244–249.

Bion, R. W. (1961). *Experiences in groups.* New York: Basic Books.

Blocher, D. (1987). *The professional counselor.* New York: Macmillan.

Blocher, D., & Biggs, D. (1983). *Counseling psychology in community settings.* New York: Springer.

Boscolo, L., Cecchin, G., Hoffman, L., & Penn, P. (1987). *Milan systemic family therapy.* New York: Basic Books.

Bowen, M. (1966). The use of family theory in clinical practice. *Comprehensive Psychiatry, 7,* 355–374.

Bowen, M. (1972). Being and becoming a family therapist. In A. Ferber, M. Mendelsohn, & A. Napier (Eds.), *The book of family therapy* (pp. 134–154). New York: Science House.

Bowen, M. (1974). Toward the differentiation of self in one's family of origin. In F. Andres & J. Lorio (Eds.), *Georgetown family symposium* (Vol. 1, pp. 170–173). New York: Science House.

Bowen, M. (1975). Family therapy after 25 years. In S. Arieti (Ed.), *American handbook of psychiatry* (Vol. 5, pp. 367–392). New York: Basic Books.

Bowen, M. (1976). Theory in the practice of psychotherapy. In P. J. Guerin (Ed.), *Family therapy: Theory and practice* (pp. 42–90). New York: Gardner Press.

Bowen, M. (1978). *Family therapy in clinical practice.* New York: Jason Aronson.

Braaten, L. J. (1974). Developmental phases of encounter groups: A critical review of models and a new proposal. *Interpersonal Development, 75,* 112–129.

Brand, S. (1974). *II Cybernetic frontiers.* New York: Random House.

Briggs, J. P., & Peat, F. D. (1984). *Looking glass universe.* New York: Simon & Schuster.

Bronowski, J. (1978). *The origins of knowledge and imagination.* New Haven, CT: Yale University Press.

Caplan, N., & Nelson, S. (1973). On being useful: The nature and consequences of psychological research on social problems. *American Psychologist, 28,* 199–211.

Capra, F. (1983). *The turning point.* New York: Bantam Books.

Carkhuff, R. (1969). *Helping and human relations* (Vol. 2). New York: Holt, Rinehart & Winston.

Castore, G. (1962). Number of verbal interrelationships as a determinant of group size. *Journal of Abnormal and Social Psychology, 64,* 456–457.

Cecchin, G. (1992). Constructing therapeutic possibilities. In S. McNamee & K. J. Gergen (Eds.), *Therapy as social construction* (pp. 86–95). Newbury Park, CA: Sage.

Churchman, C. (1979). *The systems approach and its enemies.* New York: Basic Books.

Coe, D. M., & Zimpfer, D. G. (in press). Infusing solution-oriented theory and techniques into group work. *Journal for Specialists in Group Work.*

Combs, G., & Freedman, J. (1990). Symbol, story and ceremony. New York: W. W. Norton.

Corey, G. (1995). *Theory and practice of group counseling.* Pacific Grove, CA: Brooks/ Cole.

Dell, P. (1983). From pathology to ethics. *The Family Therapy Networker, 1,* 29–64.

de Shazer, S. (1984). The death of resistance. *Family Process, 23,* 11–21.

de Shazer, S. (1985). *Keys to solutions in brief therapy.* New York: W. W. Norton.

de Shazer, S. (1991). *Putting difference to work.* New York: W. W. Norton.

de Shazer, S. (1994). *Words were originally magic.* New York: W. W. Norton.

Duhl, F., Kantor, D., & Duhl, B. (1973). Learning space and action in family therapy: A primer of sculpture. In D. Bloch (Ed.), *Techniques of family therapy.* New York: Grune and Stratton.

Dunphy, D. C. (1974). The function of fantasy in groups. In G. S. Gibbard, J. J. Hartman, & R. D. Mann (Eds.), *Analysis of groups.* San Francisco: Jossey-Bass.

Efran, J., & Lukens, S. (1985). The world according to Humberto Maturana. *The Family Therapy Networker, 9,* 23–28, 72–75.

Eliot, C. W. (Ed.). (1910). *Harvard classics scientific paper* (Vol. 38). New York: Collier.

Epston, D. (1994). Extending the conversation. *The Family Therapy Networker, 18,* 30–37, 52–53.

Fisch, R., Weakland, J., & Segal, L. (1982). *The tactics of change.* San Francisco: Jossey-Bass.

Flemons, D. (1991). *Competing distinctions.* Boston: Shambhala.

Foucault, M. (1975). *The archeology of knowledge.* London: Tavistock.

Foucault, M. (1977). *Discipline and punishment.* London: Allen Lane.

Foucault, M. (1979). *Discipline and punishment.* New York: Pantheon.

Gale, J., & Long, J. (1995). *Theoretical foundations of family therapy.* Unpublished manuscript. University of Georgia, Athens.

Gardner, J. W. (1990). *On leadership.* New York: Free Press.

Gergen, K. (1991). *The saturated self.* New York: Basic Books.

Gergen, K. (1994). Exploring the postmodern: Perils or potentials? *American Psychologist, 49,* 412–416.

Gergen, K. J. & Gergen, M. J. (1983). Narratives of the self. In T. R. Sabin & K. E. Scheibe (Eds.), *Studies in Social Identity.* New York: Praeger.

Gergen, K. J., & Kaye, J. (1992). Beyond narrative in negotiation of therapeutic meaning. In S. McNamee & K. J. Gergen (Eds.), *Therapy as social construction* (pp. 165–185). Newbury Park, CA: Sage.

Golann, S. (1988a). On second-order family therapy. *Family Process, 27,* 51–65.

Goolishian, H. (1991). The use of language in two different therapy approaches. *AAMFT Annual Conference Newsletter,* p. 1.

Goolishian, H. (Speaker). (1993). *Conversation with a blended family: A burning question* [videotape]. Master's Work Video Productions.

Guerin, P. J., & Pendagast, E. (1976). Evaluation of family systems and genograms. In P. J. Guerin, (Ed.), *Family therapy: Theory and practice* (pp. 450–464). New York: Gardner.

Haley, J. (1976). *Problem-solving therapy.* New York: Harper Colophon.

Hansen, J., Warner, R., & Smith, E. (1980). *Group counseling: Theory and practice* (2nd ed.). Chicago: Rand McNally.

Hartley, D., Roback, H., & Abramovitz, S. (1976). Deterioration effects in encounter groups. *American Psychologist, 31,* 247–255.

Hayward, J. W. (1984). *Perceiving ordinary magic.* Boston: New Science Library.

Hoffman, L. (1985). Beyond power and control. *Family Systems Medicine, 4,* 381–396.

Hoffman, L. (1993). *Exchanging voices: A collaborative approach to family therapy.* London: Karnac.

Hoffman-Hennessay, L., & Davis, J. (1993). Tekka with feathers: Talking about talking (about suicide). In S. Friedman (Ed.), *The new language of change* (pp. 345–373). New York: Guilford.

Jenkins, A. (1990). *Invitations to responsibility: The therapeutic engagement of men who are violent and abusive.* Adelaide, Australia: Dulwich Centre Publications.

Keeney, B. (1982). Not pragmatics, not aesthetics. *Family Process, 21,* 429–434.

Keeney, B. (1983). *Aesthetics of change.* New York: Guilford.

Korzybski, A. (1958). *Science and sanity: An introduction to non-Aristotelian system and general semantics* (4th ed.). Lake Shore, CT: Institute of General Semantics.

La Coursiere, R. (1974). A group method to facilitate learning during the stages of a psychiatric affiliation. *International Journal of Group Psychotherapy, 24,* 114–119.

La Coursiere, R. (1980). *The life-cycle of groups: Group development and stage theory.* New York: Human Sciences.

Laird, J. (1995). Family-centered practice in the postmodern era. *Families in Society: The Journal of Contemporary Human Services, 76,* 150–162.

Lather, P. (1986). Research as praxis. *Harvard Educational Review, 56,* 257–277.

Laube, J., & Trefz, S. (1994). Group therapy using a narrative theory framework: Application to treatment of depression. *Journal of Systemic Therapies, 13,* 29–37.

Lax, W. (1992). Postmodern thinking in clinical practice. In S. McNamee & K. J. Gergen (Eds.), *Therapy as social construction* (pp. 69–85). Newbury Park, CA: Sage.

Leavitt, H. G. (1951). Some effects of certain communication problems on group performance. *Journal of Abnormal and Social Psychology, 46,* 38–50.

Lipchik, E., & de Shazer, S. (1986). The purposeful interview. *Journal of Strategic and Systemic Therapies, 5,* 21–39.

Longino, H. (1990). *Science as social knowledge.* Princeton, NJ: Princeton University Press.

Luft, J. (1984). *Group process: An introduction to group dynamics.* San Francisco: Mayfield.

McDevitt, J. (1987). Conceptualizing therapeutic components of group counseling. *Journal for Specialists in Group Work, 12,* 76–84.

McGoldrick, M., & Gerson, R. (1985). *Genograms in family assessment.* New York: W. W. Norton.

McNamee, S., & Gergen, K. J. (1992). *Therapy as social construction.* Newbury Park, CA: Sage.

Minuchin, S. (1984). *Family kaleidoscope.* Cambridge, MA: Harvard University Press.

Morgan, A. (1995). Taking responsibility: Working with teasing and bullying in schools. *Dulwich Centre Newsletter, 2 & 3,* pp. 16–28.

Morris, J., Gawinski, B., & Joanning, H. (1994). The therapist-investigator relationship in family therapy research. *Journal of Systemic Therapies, 13,* 24–28.

Munich, R. L., & Astrachan, B. (1983). Group dynamics. In H. I. Kaplan & B. J. Sacock (Eds.), *Comprehensive group psychotherapy* (2nd ed., pp. 15–23). Baltimore: Williams and Wilkins.

O'Hanlon, W. H. (1993). Possibility therapy: From iatrogenic injury to iatrogenic healing. In S. Gilligan & R. Price (Eds.), *Therapeutic conversations* (pp. 3–17). New York: W. W. Norton.

O'Hanlon, W. H., & Weiner-Davis, M. (1989). *In search of solutions: A new direction in psychotherapy.* New York: Guilford.

Plas, J. M. (1986). *Systems psychology in the schools.* New York: Pergamon.

Rorty, R. (1989). *Contingency, irony, and solidarity.* Cambridge: Cambridge University Press.

Roth, S., & Epston, D. (1996). Developing externalizing conversations: An exercise. *Journal of Systemic Therapies, 15,* 5–12.

Sarason, S. (1981). *Psychology misdirected.* New York: Free Press.

Satir, V. (1967a). *Conjoint family therapy* (rev. ed.). Palo Alto, CA: Science and Behavior Books.

Satir, V. (1967b). A family of angels. In J. Haley & L. Hoffman (Eds.), *Techniques of family therapy* (pp. 97–173). New York: Basic Books.

Satir, V. (1971). The family as a treatment unit. In J. Haley (Ed.), *Changing families* (pp. 127–132). New York: Grune & Stratton.

Satir, V. (1972). *Peoplemaking.* Palo Alto, CA: Science and Behavior Books.

Satir, V. (1978). *Your many faces.* Millbrae, CA: Celestial Arts.

Satir, V. (1982). The therapist and family therapy: Process model. In A. Horne & M. Ohlsen (Eds.), *Family counseling and therapy* (pp. 12–42). Itasca, IL: F. E. Peacock.

Satir, V. M., & Baldwin, M. (1983). *Satir step by step: A guide to creating change in families.* Palo Alto, CA: Science and Behavior Books.

Satir, V., Stachowiak, J., & Taschman, H. (1977). *Helping families to change.* New York: Jason Aronson.

Selekman, M. (1991). The solution-oriented parenting group. *Journal of Systemic and Strategic Therapies, 10,* 36–49.

Shepherd, C. R. (1964). *Small groups.* Scranton, PA: Chandler.

Simon, R. (1972). Sculpting the family. *Family Process, 11,* 49–51.

Simon, R. (1989). Reaching out to life. *The Family Therapy Networker, 13,* 37–43.

Stewart, K., & Amundson, J. (1995). The ethical postmodernist: Or not everything is relative all at once. *Journal of Systemic Therapies, 14,* 70–78.

Tuckman, B. W. (1965). Developmental sequence in small groups. *Psychological Bulletin, 63,* 384–399.

von Glasersfeld, E. (1979). The control of perception and the construction of reality. *Dialectica, 33,* 37–50.

von Glasersfeld, E. (1984). An introduction to radical constructivism. In P. Watzlawick (Ed.), *The invented reality* (pp. 17–40). New York: W. W. Norton.

Walter, J., & Peller, J. (1992). *Becoming solution-focused in brief therapy.* New York: Bruner/Mazel.

Watts, A. (1968). *Divine madness.* Boulder: Sounds True Recordings.

Watts, A. (1972). *The book.* New York: Vintage.

Watzlawick, P. (1978). *The language of change.* New York: W. W. Norton.

Watzlawick, P. (1990). *Munchhausen's pigtail.* New York: W. W. Norton.

Watzlawick, P., Beavin, J., & Jackson, D. (1967). *Pragmatics of human communication.* New York: W. W. Norton.

Watzlawick, P., Weakland, J., & Fisch, R. (1974). *Change: Principles of problem formation and problem resolution.* New York: W. W. Norton.

*Webster's collegiate dictionary.* (1995). New York: Random House.

White, M. (1991). Deconstruction and therapy. *Dulwich Centre Newsletter, 3,* 21–40.

White, M. (1995). Schools as communities of acknowledgment. *Dulwich Centre Newsletter, 2 & 3,* 51–66.

White, M., & Epston, D. (1990). *Narrative means to therapeutic ends.* New York: W. W. Norton.

Winderman, L. (1989). Generation of human meaning key to Galveston paradigm: An interview with Harlene Anderson & Harold Goolishian. *Family Therapy News, 20,* 11–12.

Yalom, I. D. (1975). *The theory and practice of group psychotherapy* (2nd ed.). New York: Basic Books.

Zurcher, L. A., Jr. (1969). Stages of development in poverty program neighborhood committees. *Journal of Applied Behavioral Science, 5,* 223–251.

# Author Index

# Subject Index

159